~~~~~~~~~~~~~~~

Spiritual Thoughts

By Rod Durost

~~~~~~~~~~~~~~~

Copyright Year: 2007

Copyright Notice: by Rod Durost. All rights reserved.

The above information forms this copyright notice:

© *2007 by Rod Durost. All rights reserved.*

ISBN 978-0-6151-8092-2

ID: 1470129

www.lulu.com

Dear Reader,

This compilation was originally produced by the author to put his thoughts and feelings into words for his family. He completed this project by listening to nature and the Lord on long walks. This project was started in 2005 and finished in the spring of 2007. He had said when he reached a hundred pages he would stop. He did not stop at a hundred obviously.

With a good church to study and interpret the bible, this project was developed. As he produced this project, he found it could help others, not just his family. He has been asked more than a few times, "How did you come up with this?" His reply has been, "None of the words are mine. The Lord sent these words through me."

As you read this compilation, you will notice the author's faith and his wife's faith evolve to a higher state. Through these teachings, his son has found The Lord and is learning of His teachings through prayer and bible study. Only hope, prayer, faith, and persistence will bring the rest of the family to the Lord.

The author has never wanted to make a profit from any compilation dealing with the Lord. The Lord's word is free, and so should his servant's words about Him. That is the reasoning behind this project's price as being strictly the cost of the materials to put it together.

The author would hope the reader would find the true path, using this project as a template. His family would hope the reader would find this project as interesting and heart moving as they have.

Love in Christ,

Harold Durost

Spiritual Thoughts – Notes of Interest

Pg 8   **Anger Prov. 15:1** was used when your mother spoke to a young man of his responsibilities to his girlfriend & their two children.

                 As he tried to beat your mom out with loud talk your mother softened her tone & brought the conversation back to normal.

                 The girlfriend learned how to speak to her boyfriend without shouting.

Pg 11   **A Gift from God** is about Lucas being born

Pg 17   **An Unkind Word** refers to something I said about your mother & was revealed when we went thru heart cleansing classes.

Pg 21   **The Rain of Many Days** occurred one spring when several roads & homes were destroyed.

Pg 31   **Two Hearts** refer to your mom & me after we had taken the heart cleansing classes

Pg 49   **Working for God** the retirement benefits are out of this world. He gets the glory, & we get the fun.

Pg 51   **His Day** see page 28

Pg 61   **Little Voices** is about a person in our church who was sexually abused, gang raped, & involved in witchcraft - all before adulthood. Now she has over 14 different personalities who live inside her. These little girls come out sometimes and talk with us.

Pg 62	**Moment by Moment**	Doris E. is a member of our assembly
Pg 79	**At Mom's Passing**	I wrote this after Tennessee.
Pg 87	**Storms**	C. Noble is part of our assembly
Pg 88	**Thank You, Lord**	is about the Dad
Pg 110	**The Days of My Conversion**	is about the Dad
Pg 118	**Pity Her**	is about a neighbor
Pg 126	**From Christine S.**	She is part of our assembly
Pg 156	**Hollywood Hype verses Scripture Sense**	is part of the reason I gave away or sold 2,500 movies
Pg 157	**The Enemy Within**	written according to actual events
Pgs 163	**Sermon on the Mount**	all the details we need to live the Christian life. It is our manual in order to be Christian (Christ-Like)

Evolution

Emma, my partner for life, made a very good point. If we evolved from apes, why are they still here?

~~~~~~~~~~~~~~~

The Root of All Evil

When I was in my twenties, I thought I had been called to preach. I had already seen the miracles of God; $9 a week for groceries; a small amount of food which fills you up; money coming to us to buy fuel when we had no money to buy it; frugal living without feeling deprived.

One day I was called into our pastor's study. He told me that when I got to college, they would teach me how to get more money from the congregation, so I need not worry about money after school. "Congregations like to keep their pastors poor, to keep them humble."

I was devastated. Money was not a priority to me, leading others to Christ was. I soon found myself without a church and drifting away from God. It took me over twenty years to find my way back. Thank you Lord for your patience and mercy.

~~~~~~~~~~~~~~~~~~~

Power

Do you know the power of Jesus? Why would you go through life living day by day without using the very tool given to you by salvation? By letting Him control your life, you are happier, with less problems & more love in your life.

~~~~~~~~~~~~~~~~~~~~~~~~

Spiritual Thoughts

TV or not TV

When we first got married, we decided because we read a lot, not to buy a TV. Because people could not believe that we would ever survive, we were given three that year. Now we keep one in the house, we just don't have it hooked up to cable or an antenna.

~~~~~~~~~~~~~~~~~

The Bible

Read the Word of God,

Eternity is a long time to be wrong!

~~~~~~~~~~~

From: The Christ of the Mount
By: E. Stanley Jones

Jesus came not to get men into heaven,

But to get heaven into men;

Not get men out of hell,

But to get hell out of men.

~~~~~~~~~~~~~~~~~~~~

The Church Building

Is the building for the glory & purposes of God,

Or the ego of man?

~~~~~~~~~~~~~~~~~~~~~~~~

Brotherly Love in the Old Testament

Starting with Exodus chapters 21 - 23 we find the love of God.

Chapter 21 - faithful servants

Chapter 22 - duty to neighbors, strangers, widows, children

Chapter 23 - do good to enemies, poor,

The Old Testament God is the same as the New Testament God.

~~~~~~~~~~~~~~~~~~~~

Sin

Sin will keep you from the Bible.

The Bible will keep you from sin.

~~~~~~~~~~~~~~~~~~~~

Possessions

If you steal my possessions, I can replace them either with money or memories,

But you can never steal my salvation for it is a gift of God!!!

~~~~~~~~~~~~~~~~~~~~

Solomon said

The things which God has commanded are proved by experience to be best for men, and the essence of human wisdom is in keeping God's commandments.

~~~~~~~~~~~~~~~~

Spiritual Thoughts

Ashamed on Judgment Day

While in mediation I realized that our friends & neighbors didn't know about Jesus. I thought if I am standing before God on judgment day, I can only hang my head in shame, when they are sentenced to an eternity without Jesus. And then they remark, "Rodney, why didn't you tell us?" I immediately set to work to let them know. I sent them all the truth about their religion, Catholicism, and the simple plan of salvation.

Don't be ashamed of Jesus. We have the greatest gift that God can give and we need to share it. I would rather people hate me for preaching Jesus, than to have God's rebuke for hiding the truth

Gal. 4:16 Am I therefore become your enemy, because I tell you the truth?

~~~~~~~~~~~~~~~

Hate

After some time in my turning back to God, I found my closeness to God becoming distant. By examining myself, I found hate for my stepfather was at the cause of this hold on my spiritual life. I asked God for forgiveness, and then added David to my daily prayers in hope he would receive salvation.

An opportunity came to visit David, who lives at least two days away, and I took it. On my arrival, within the first two hours, I found myself in his kitchen with a fresh baked biscuit, country fried ham, and a cup of coffee. I asked him about Mom's health, his health, and then I asked, "Are you saved?"

He said he was saved & baptized, but he had some sin in his life. I counseled and comforted the man as best I could with God's help.

I had been at this man's house before, but this was the most joyful, for I knew I would see him again in the New Kingdom. Now, I would only have to pray for his health.

I shook his hand for the first time the day I left, and said, "Thank you."

The benefits were immediate: relief, joy, a burden lifted, a closer walk with God, more spiritual guidance.

Give up hate for love & concern, the benefits are amazing.

~~~~~~~~~~~~~~~~~

Sin that holds you back

I was reading a book "Victorious Living" by E. Stanley Jones, when I found God speaking to me.

Even though I had talked to David (my stepfather) about salvation, I had not confessed to him my past sins toward him. Immediately, I wrote him a letter in which I told him of my past feelings of hate and deceitfulness and then asked for his forgiveness.

Then I went to God in prayer. My life became brighter.

~~~~~~~~~~~~~~~~

Man's wisdom verses God's

How can a piece of clay be smarter than the potter? How can an ear of corn be smarter than the planter of the field? Yet man tries to be wiser than his Creator. Man assumes himself to be wise, yet he is more foolish than one who does not toil before winter and therefore has nothing to sustain him during the cold, and dies of hunger and the cold.

(Continued Next Page)

Spiritual Thoughts

Yet, I know who sustains me in time of trouble, and who guards my riches in the next life. It is my Lord God!!!

Can man calm the sea or heal the sick with only a word? No, only my Creator has the power to do these things. Only God can control nature, heal, and save His people from certain death. Only God can save us from the destruction which is coming and only God would send His Son to die for us.

Man is but a speck in the universe, but God cares about this speck, so He allows man to think himself equal to the Creator only until He shall come again and every knee shall bow and **every man** shall know **He is the Lord!!!**

~~~~~~~~~~~~

Christian

It means "Christ-like" How close can we get? As men we are born with a sinful nature. It destroys us, unless we attempt to ask God for help in keeping from it. The first step is to accept Christ. Then on a daily walk with God, we keep sin out of our life. Only we can make the choice of a walk with God or to live without Him.

~~~~~~~~~~~~

Revelation interpretation

Three words - let God lead. There are many books on this one book of the Bible. There are four different ways to interpret it. The best way I think, is for you to read and then ask God to help you understand its meaning. Who knows more about scripture than the author?

~~~~~~~~~~~

Idol worship

An idol is anything you place in importance above God. Some examples: watching TV, playing video games, collecting every James Bond movie, or any activity that God would not approve of, yet, it pleases you.

~~~~~~~~~~~~~~~~~~~~~~

Pilgrim

I'm just a pilgrim in search of a city,

I want a mansion, a harp, and a crown

"Mansion on a Hill Top"

I am not here long, so I need to get His work done so I can go home.

~~~~~~~~~~~~~~~

God's importance

Is God someone you think of on Sunday and maybe occasionally during the week?

Or is God someone you walk with daily, guiding your steps and catching you when you fall?

~~~~~~~~~~~~~~~~~

All That Matters
Micah Henson
2004 by Nolink Music
Centergy Music/BMI

(Continued Next Page)

Spiritual Thoughts

As sung by the Nelons

For He is all that matters

When this thing is over

We've crossed death's cold waters

We'll see more clearly

We'll see that really He's it.

~~~~~~~~~~~~~

Anger

Proverbs 15:1 A soft answer turneth away wrath: but grievous words stir up anger.

To turn a heated conversation, try speaking softly with reason.

~~~~~~~~~~~~~

They Saw

They saw the plagues in Egypt, but they rebelled against God.

They saw the red sea divided and walked in the midst, but they rebelled against God.

They found manna from heaven, but they rebelled against God.

They searched out the land, but complained because they didn't trust in God.

They saw Jesus heal the sick & raise the dead, but they wouldn't believe in Him.

    We saw none of these things, but we believe in Him.

~~~~~~~~~~~~~~~~~

God's laws

In Leviticus 18&19 we find the adherence to all that God wants us to live by. These have not changed. They only enforce the over 700 commands in the New Testament. The greatest commandment that is mentioned is LOVE. This one has not diminished for thousands of years. It is sometimes hard to love your enemy, but God says we must. If we truly love those who hate us, they will either become a friend, or they will ignore us. What do we have to lose?

~~~~~~~~~~~~

It's a powerful thing.

It is easy to become a person who wishes to have everyone believe as they do.

Having the love of Jesus within, and the desire to share it, is a powerful thing.

We want to allow Jesus to come into everyone's life.

The problem is that those who don't know Him often don't know the feeling of genuine love.

You can lead someone to church, but you can't make them believe. It's a choice.

You need to pray for that person's realization of the truth, Jesus is love.

~~~~~~~~~~~~

Spiritual Thoughts

When you pray

Do you pray everyday?

Do you pray just for you & your immediate family?

Do you pray for thanks?

Do you uplift God?

Do you have a list of prayer requests & people to pray for?

Do you pray during the day for things you do or think about?

God doesn't mind listening.

~~~~~~~~~~~~~~

I didn't have time to accept Jesus

When I died suddenly, I didn't have time.

When the accident took my life, I didn't have time.

When I was too busy with life, I didn't have time.

When they came to my door to tell me about Jesus, I didn't have time.

While at church, I was thinking of other things, and I didn't have time.

When Jesus came in all His glory, I wasn't ready.

Take time now! Tomorrow may be too late!

~~~~~~~~~~~~~~~~~

More

There is more to life than you can see.

There is love, inner peace, contentment.

All are found in Jesus.

We can not see Him, but we believe.

We can not see heaven, but we know it exists.

We have not seen eternity, but we have hope.

~~~~~~~~~~~~~~~~~~~~

A gift from God

At 9:30 p.m. he came into our lives.

He was small, in stress, & new to the world.

He had a great future before him.

He would be loved, cuddled, and spoken softly to.

He had a little patch of hair, blue eyes, & much promise.

His name is Lucas, and he is my new grandchild.

He, like my other two grandchildren, is a much welcomed addition.

~~~~~~~~~~~~~~~~~~~

In less than 100 years . . .

We have perfected the automobile.

We have put men on the moon.

We have perfected air travel.

(Continued Next Page)

Spiritual Thoughts

We have built devises for storing millions of pieces of information that takes up very little space.

We have advanced in technology & science,

Lest we become proud of our accomplishments, let us remember who made us & the universe. God still owns all of creation. He has left it in our care. We better not forget who we work for.

~~~~~~~~~~~~~

Numbers 15:39

...remember all the commandments of the LORD, and do them; and that ye seek not after your own heart and your own eyes, after which ye use to go a whoring:

~~~~~~~~~~~~~~~~~

A sea of want

I once left His walk to pursue my own desires. I was a drift upon a sea of want. Never was I satisfied, because the harder I worked to achieve my goals, the more I was unsatisfied. At last I found Him again, and gave up all to follow Him. He became the principal one I wished to please. My possessions became His. My desires became only for His service. My thoughts were only how to serve Him & others better.

~~~~~~~~~~~~~~

Spiritual Maturity

It is an on going process. It takes us closer to God. It finds our faults, sins, shortcomings and seeks to make us better. As we cast off the unwanted things of man we find peace, contentment, and closer to our goal of being Christ-like. It is not a step as much as a way of living. Making God the central portion of our life is not a burden, but a relief of worldly problems.

~~~~~~~~~~~~~~~~~

Sacrifice
What would you be willing to give up for God?
He gave us His Son.

~~~~~~~~~~~~~~~~

Idolatry

We worship money, possessions, movie stars, our own lusts. None of this gives us as much pleasure as serving an infinite God. The one takes away our future. The other builds that future. Life is brief. A short service to God brings an eternity of blessedness.

~~~~~~~~~~~~~~~

Our Father which art in heaven

When you were a child, did you ever have this conversation with yourself?

"What would Dad think of me doing this?"

Well, you are a child of God. What would He say about what you watch, do, or say?

~~~~~~~~~~~

Spiritual Thoughts

The Reign of Christ

His reign must be in our conscious & sub-conscious mind.

His reign must be in our daily life and not just Sunday

His reign must be 24 hours a day and not just at prayer time.

He must have complete reign or conflict will dwell within you.

Who do you serve?

~~~~~~~~~~

Trials & Tribulation

Deut. 8:2 And thou shalt remember all the way which the LORD thy God led thee these forty years in the wilderness, to humble thee, *and* to prove thee, **to know what *was* in thine heart,** whether thou wouldest keep his commandments, or not.

If you go through a bad time, do you wonder whether God is watching over you? Perhaps He is testing your faith and what is in your heart.

~~~~~~~~~~~~

Continued...

Out of the Land of Bondage you brought us.

In the wilderness of Life we traveled.

The sun was hot upon our heads,

The sand was hot beneath our feet

We threw down the idols of possessions, self, & worry.

We embraced your laws and they were written on our hearts.

You provided our food & raiment.

Through trials, tests, & tribulation you proved us worthy.

We worshiped and served you all of our earthly lives.

Now as we cross Jordan, we see that bright land of hope.

We can now see the possessions laid up in store for us.

We can now serve our Lord all of our days.

And we can praise the Almighty for eternity.

~~~~~~~~~~~~~~~

Belief

1John 3:23 And this is his commandment, That we should believe on the name of his Son Jesus Christ, and love one another, as he gave us commandment.

It is a choice and a commandment to believe on Jesus & to love everyone. We must believe in Jesus and accept Him or face eternity without Him. Jesus is The Life, The Way, & The Truth.

~~~~~~~~~~~~~~~

Purging

Do you ask for forgiveness from your mind or from the heart?

You may purge your mind of a sin, but the heart may hold onto it.

Satan uses this against you and you feel miserable.

(Continued Next Page)

Spiritual Thoughts

Ask God to rid you of sin, renounce Satan's desire to use it against you.

And then ask God to submit to His desire for you.

And finally find a verse that will help you remember God's desire for you.

~~~~~~~~~~~

Believe It or Not
The Nelons

Believe it or not I believe He's coming again!

Shout it from the housetops

Tell everyone you can

The trumpets gonna sound so loud

We'll be called to Gloryland

~~~~~~~~~~~~~~

Charity

Mat 25:34-40

> 34 Then shall the King say unto them on his right hand, Come, ye blessed of my Father, inherit the kingdom prepared for you from the foundation of the world:
>
> 35 For I was hungry, and ye gave me meat: I was thirsty, and ye gave me drink: I was a stranger, and ye took me in
>
> 36 Naked and ye clothed me: I was sick, and ye visited me: I was in prison, and ye came unto me.
>
> 37 Then shall the righteous answer him, saying, Lord, when saw we thee hungry, and fed *thee*? Or thirsty, and gave *thee* drink?
>
> 38 When saw we thee a stranger, and took *thee* in? Or naked, and clothed *thee*?
>
> 39 Or when saw we thee sick, or in prison, and came unto thee?

40 And the King shall answer and say unto them, Verily I say unto you, Inasmuch as ye have done *it* unto one of the least of these my brethren, ye have done *it* unto me.

Can there be enough love in the world?

~~~~~~~~~~~~~

Gossip

Speak kindly of others,

God is listening.

~~~~~~~~~~~~~

God's correction

Deut. 8:5 Thou shalt also consider in thine heart, that, as a man chasteneth his son, *so* the LORD thy God chasteneth thee.

If you are a child of God, expect correction to help you to grow spiritually.

~~~~~~~~~~~~~

An Unkind Word

It was said many years before.

He didn't know the pain he caused.

She told him what he said and her feeling of being unloved.

(Continued Next Page)

He said he was sorry for her pain.

He asked for forgiveness.

She forgave him

They fell into each others arms in tears.

The distance between them became smaller.

They found new love.

~~~~~~~~~~~~~~~

So little time

So many strangers.

So many neighbors.

So many friends.

So many relatives.

So little time to tell them about Jesus.

~~~~~~~~~~~

Constant Battles

Every time temptation is present,

When asked if God exists by a person

Who is better acquainted with the enemy?

When you keep back promises to God because of self.

Keeping secrets from your spouse.

Dealing in half truths.

These are <u>all</u> things of spiritual warfare.

~~~~~~~~~~~~

Eternal

Spoken of two thousand years before He came.

Spoken of two thousand years after He left.

Things come and go,

But our Jesus is still the same.

He only becomes sweeter as we grow in Him.

~~~~~~~~

Defending the Faith

In defending the faith, do we also defend self?

We must be careful of asserting our beliefs to others.

That we do not trample God's work.

Self, ego, & pride work for the enemy if not checked.

~~~~~~~~~~~~~~~~

Spiritual Thoughts

The Test

Am I truthful?

Am I honest?

Am I pure?

Am I easily offended or am I loving?

Am I selfish or am I consecrated?

~~~~~~~~~~~~

The Two Witnesses

In Revelation 11, we find two witnesses who in the last three and a half years of the tribulation are preaching the gospel. They are destroyed by Satan and mankind rejoices.

We are sometimes ridiculed, ignored, or persecuted because we preach Jesus. The Truth is the Truth. It can be ignored, laughed at, or spoken against, but it doesn't change. It endures forever!

~~~~~~~~~

What is holding you back?

I don't want to be part of organized religion.

I am much too busy.

I don't want to change my life style.

I have things I don't want to give up.

My spouse won't accept the change.

What is stopping you from accepting Jesus?

~~~~~~~~~~

The Rain of Many Days

The rain falls on the rich and the poor.

The rain falls on the just and the unjust

It causes the streams to become rivers.

It causes people to flee their homes and their possessions

It causes us to seek God's divine reasoning.

If we lose possessions because of the rain,

Are we sorrowful?

Does not God own everything?

We look to God for answers.

We know of tests and tribulations.

It gives the unjust a chance to seek God for answers.

Should we ask God to stop the rain,

Or ask for His protection,

And seek His will and His plan?

~~~~~~~~~~~~~~~~~~~~~~

Victorious Living
E. Stanley Jones
I sail with Thy hand on the helm of my life
and everything under Thy control

~~~~~~~~~~~

Spiritual Thoughts

Rom 8:31 . . . If God *be* for us, who *can be* against us?

Not mankind.

Not the government.

Not Satan.

Nothing period!

~~~~~~~~~~~

Marriage

A man should not rule over his wife.

A man should rule with his wife.

Decisions should be a compromise by both husband & wife.

Eve came from Adam's side not his foot.

~~~~~~~~~~~

When Will It Stop?

For thousands of years

The enemy has sown lies, deceptions, fear.

The enemy fights, but without success,

For he can not win.

It has been foretold who will win the battle.

Truth clings on even in adversity.

When all seems lost for good,

God triumphs, for He is mightier than all

Fear not the enemy, he will be defeated.

~~~~~~~~~~~~

The Da Vinci Code

A novel turned into a lie.

Though many will believe this lie,

They do so in order to boost their inner feelings for self.

At most it is an interesting tale of fiction.

It is not the truth,

That can only be found in scripture

If we make Jesus as human as we,

We lose all hope of salvation.

Would all of His disciples die a cruel death for a lie?

Would you?

~~~~~~~~~~~~

The Da Vinci Deception
By Erwin W. Lutzer
As fabrications go, "The Da Vinci Code"
is right up there with Elvis sightings.

~~~~~~~~~~~~

Spiritual Thoughts

2Timothy 4:3-4

> 3 For the time will come when they will not endure sound doctrine; but after their own lusts shall they heap to themselves teachers, having itching ears;
>
> 4 And they shall turn away *their* ears from the truth, and shall be turned unto fables.

~~~~~~~~~~~~~

Rescue the Perishing

By Fanny J. Crosby

Down in the human heart, crushed by the tempter,

Feelings lie buried that grace can restore;

Touched by a loving heart, wakened by kindness,

Chords that are broken will vibrate once more.

~~~~~~~~~~~~~

Mind Vs Heart

The mind says:

> Take it! They don't pay you enough!
>
> Fudge a little on your taxes, everyone does it.
>
> They'll never miss just one.
>
> They made the mistake, why should I tell them?
>
> The wife doesn't need to know!

The heart says:

> Shame on you!

>   Render unto Caesar that which is Caesar's!
>
>   Stealing is wrong!
>
>   Honesty is the best policy!
>
>   Don't keep secrets in your marriage!

Listen to your heart; It just may be the voice of God.

~~~~~~~~~~

Sin

You can not hide sin from God.

It will find you out.

~~~~~~~~~~~~~~~

Miracles

Talk to an unbeliever about God's miracles in your life,

And they will roll their eyes, and consider you with disbelief.

Talk with a believer about God's miracles in your life,

And they will nod their head in agreement.

What a difference in living everyday, expecting a miracle.

~~~~~~~~~~~~~~~

Spiritual Thoughts

The Road Less Traveled

Walking the road less traveled,

I commune with God each day.

I find solitude most refreshing

As God has His way.

My days are not hurried,

So it gives me time to see,

All that God has in life,

For someone like me.

The wood speaks so softly,

And the breeze gently blows.

I know not where I'm heading,

Yet my God always knows.

As I end my journey,

I will finally see,

My precious, loving Jesus,

The one who died for me.

~~~~~~~~~~~~~

Serving God

Service to the Master.

Service to a friend.

Service for a life time.

Or service to the end.

The rewards out weigh the service.

~~~~~~~~~~~~~~~

24 Hour Access

In the 20th Century, business came up with the idea of "24 hour access". This was prevalent in finance, banking, medical, & service.

God has for centuries had "24 hour access". He has been there for: comfort, protection, strength, & abundance.

The difference is - **you can always trust God.** He will never tell you anything but the truth. He will always be there when you need Him. His wisdom is above reproach. His power is greater than any on earth.

~~~~~~~~~~~~~~~

What if. . .?

.each business in America started their day with prayer?

.each business advertised only the truth?

.each business concentrated on quality and fair trade?

(Continued Next Page)

Spiritual Thoughts

.each business was only interested in customer satisfaction, not profits?

.each business was interested in the employee's quality of life?

.each business practiced sound biblical teachings?

~~~~~~~~~~~~~

You Can Trust in Him

For Abraham & Sarah in their golden years He built a mighty nation.

For Moses, He brought plagues upon Egypt to free Israel from bondage.

For Moses, He opened the earth and took away the accusers of Moses.

For Joshua, He held back the waters of Jordan so Israel could pass over.

For Joshua, He destroyed Israel's enemies with hail.

For us, He gave us salvation through the sacrifice of His Son.

~~~~~~~~~~~~~

The Tithe

Do you tithe the net income or the gross?

Do you realize that it all belongs to God?

"In the beginning God created the heavens and the earth".

Do you take from the tithe to do that thing that is supposed to be an offering?

Do you not know that God will give you back even more than you will give?

A tithe is God's.

An offering is from the heart.

Give with a glad heart, that God may bless you with His love & His bounty.

~~~~~~~~~~~~~

Religiously

Do you. . .

>Exercise religiously?

>Call a relative or a friend religiously?

>Take medication or vitamins religiously?

>Mow your yard religiously?

>Stay on your diet religiously?

>Go to church religiously?

>Serve God religiously?

~~~~~~~~~~~~~~~

What Position Is the Transmission?

Some church members are in "park".

They are saved & waiting for death or The Lord's Coming.

Some church members are in "neutral".

They come infrequently in order to catch up with the gossip.

Some church members are in "drive".

They do what is necessary to be in acceptance of their fellow members.

Some church members are in "drive with their foot on the accelerator"

They are on fire for the Lord and want to do service for Him.

~~~~~~~~~~~~

Spiritual Thoughts

Priorities

God or the game?

God or money?

God or things?

God or image?

God or self?

~~~~~~~~~~~~~

God's Children

We don't always know why God sends us problem people.

His ways are not our ways.

Maybe they need guidance.

Maybe they are being primed for future service.

Maybe they or we are being tested.

Whatever the reason, we need to help & pray for them.

Our job is simple, do God's will.

~~~~~~~~~~~~~

Man Is Like a Child

He wants his toys - motorcycle, boat, old car.

He likes his tinker toys - old car, wood shop, the earth.

He has difficulties in control & attitudes toward job, self, women.

Ego is his pride & hurt.

He wants to be in control instead of the Creator.

Man is complex, yet so simple.

~~~~~~~~~~~~

Two Hearts

Two hearts meeting for the first time.

Two hearts soon becoming one.

Two hearts becoming entwined.

Two hearts rejoicing in new lives.

Two hearts going through each day with life's goals.

Two hearts working to raise a family.

Two hearts seeing their family separate into many different families.

Two hearts starting to drift apart.

Two hearts finding a renewed interest in God.

Two hearts seeing Jesus and forgiving each other for past sins.

Two hearts finding each other in a new way.

Two hearts communicating and loving each other again.

Two hearts forever entwined and serving Jesus.

~~~~~~~~~~

Spiritual Thoughts

Sequencing

Is it important that we know the exact sequence of events that will happen at the rapture?

Or that we know that it will happen?

~~~~~~~~~~~~~

God

He is who He is because He is.

If one man were to attain all the world's knowledge, he could never be as wise as Him.

~~~~~~~~~~

The Throne Room

We enter with heads bowed.

We fall on our knees before the King.

We praise our most benevolent Protector.

We ask for forgiveness for wrongs we have done.

We seek His wisdom.

We ask things for others.

We ask things for ourselves.

We leave in humble adoration,

For we know He will serve us far greater, than we can serve ourselves

~~~~~~~~~~~~~~~

They Are Many

They all live within one heart.

They all have tales of woe.

They each speak of a time when they were frightened or hurt.

They are children seeking a way to ease that woe.

Then they find Jesus.

He eases their pain & makes the man of lies to flee.

Jesus teaches them to be unafraid and dependent on Him.

Jesus becomes their savior.

Jesus becomes their friend.

The heart is healed and the person becomes whole

~~~~~~~~~~~~~~

The Untruth

It starts as a small innocent lie.

It gains strength and grows.

It deceives the ignorant and the learned.

It becomes the damning of souls.

It is the work of the enemy.

(Continued Next Page)

It so wrings out the wine of truth,

That one will not believe the real truth.

Woe unto man that will grasp the enemies' lies,

And will not accept the true gospel.

~~~~~~~~~~~~

Joel 3:13-14 Put ye in the sickle, for the harvest is ripe: come, get you down; for the press is full, the fats overflow; for their wickedness *is* great.

14 Multitudes, multitudes in the valley of decision: for the day of the LORD *is* near in the valley of decision.

~~~~~~~~~~~~

The King is Coming
Gather Music Co.

Oh the King is coming

The King is coming

I just heard the trumpets sounding

And now His face I see. . .

Oh the king is coming

The King is coming

Praise God, He's coming for me

~~~~~~~~~~

He is My Refuge

Storm clouds surround me

Hard rain beats upon my skin,

Thunder drowns out my speech,

And lightning strikes before me.

Yet I am unafraid,

For this morning I prepared.

I fed my soul with His word,

I closed my eyes to listen for His voice,

I talked with Him

Though storm clouds gather,

His truth still stands against it.

His strength sustains me as winds blow and rain falls.

I fear not the lightning, for I know He will shield me.

My words often fall on deaf ears,

Yet I will proclaim the gospel of Jesus,

For should just one soul believe,

Then my mission is a success.

(Continued Next Page)

Spiritual Thoughts

God's kingdom will advance

With or without the choices of men.

God will have the victory,

And His truth will win out.

Please, dear souls listen,

For His voice is softly calling.

He calls for all to enter into His rest and safety.

Would you please answer His call?

~~~~~~~~~

Psalms 55:22 Cast thy burden upon the LORD, and he shall sustain thee: he shall never suffer the righteous to be moved.

~~~~~~~~~~~

Psalms 23:1 <u>The Lord is my Shepard, I shall not want.</u>

~~~~~~~~~~

Victorious Living
By E. Stanley Jones

Jesus said two astonishing things.

Matt. 26:26 . . . Take, eat; this is my body.

He offered His body for humanity to feed upon. I would not dim the idea of the atonement in these words. That idea is there and we are grateful. But is this idea not there too: that He offered to feed men on the way He treated His body, the way He made his bodily appetites subserve the purposes of the kingdom, the way He sublimated His sex impulses, and the way He kept pure in act and in thought - in short, does He not offer to men His whole bodily victory? Feed upon that fact, He says.

Matt. 26:27-28

27 . . . Drink ye all of it; For this is my blood of the new testament,
28 Also, was not this idea there? He was beginning a new blood stream, a new hereditary of a higher race, and that now we can have the source of our blood hereditary, not in the tainted, contaminated past of which we are the unwilling inheritors, but in a new pure, untainted source of inherited life.

They both go together. I shall keep myself pure today, by feeding on His victory, that some may feed on mine.

When tempted today you must say, "No, that would make me unfit to say to anyone, "Drink of my life and of my new line." No, for their sakes I sanctify myself -yes, my very blood, that I may be able to feed, not poison, this and coming generations.

~~~~~~~~~~

Spiritual Thoughts

THE JONES' PRAYER

O Christ, of the pure body, make me like that. May no impure thought or deed this day incapacitate me for offering my victory to tempted souls. O Christ, I thank you that you can offer to me your blood and that I belong to the new hereditary. Help me to be worthy of such a line. And help me to hold within me the dignity of the life to which I belong. Keep me pure and may a new humble pride posses me.

~~~~~~~~~~~~~~~~~~

Luke22:19-20 And he took bread, and gave thanks, and broke *it,* and gave unto them, saying, This is my body which is given for you: this do in remembrance of me.

20 Likewise also the cup after supper, saying, This cup *is* the new testament in my blood, which is shed for you.

~~~~~~~~~~~~~~~~~~

She's My Soul Mate

I spent the whole day in spiritual turmoil.

I made plans that were drastic in nature.

I prayed for an answer.

Then she came home at the end of the day.

She looked at my plans.

Then she told me of her plans.

She made more sense than I.

She eased my mind and helped me to think more clearly.

Together we formulated a plan.

She helps to calm my spirit & gives me love.

Thank you, Lord!

~~~~~~~~~~~

It's His Stuff

We had a yard sale. I decided that I would rid myself of everything that would hurt my witness for God. Since God owns everything (Gen. 1:1) there was nothing that was in my house that belonged to me. Holding nothing back meant that when several people asked for an item that wasn't for sale, we interrupted that to mean that God wanted us to get rid of it. It was the most money we had ever seen for a yard sale. All of my problem witness items went the first day. It was a very profitable Friday & Saturday.

We remembered to give God all the glory & honor & tithe. As Brother David Smith is fond of saying, "He gets the glory. We get the fun." AMEN!

If you work for God, He will work for you.

~~~~~~~~~~~

Our Enemy

He deals in half truths.

He deals in lies.

He causes pain & suffering.

His aim is to hurt.

(Continued Next Page)

Spiritual Thoughts

His aim is to deceive.

When we feel his work in our lives,

We cry out to God.

Satan then is defeated.

Maybe because we are successful in God's Kingdom,

We are hurting Satan's.

Praise be to God for His truthfulness, protection, & victory!

~~~~~~~~~~~~~~~~

Family

I see them every now and then,

They seem so strange to me.

I talk with them, but they try not to listen.

I still love them, but I no longer have their desires.

They serve different gods.

They are my old family.

They have no desire, to serve my Lord.

They see Him as a hindrance to this life.

They turn away at the mention of His name.

They find no solace in His grace.

They seek not His wisdom or His salvation.

They only see the present and not the eternity that is.

I see them every Sunday.

They fill my heart with joy.

If I should meet them on the street,

I find such love for them.

It is because we have like thoughts.

It is because my new family serves the same God.

~~~~~~~~~~~

Wealth

Which would you rather have?

Wealth on earth or wealth in heaven?

~~~~~~~~~~~~~~~

The Angel's Warning

Revelation 14:8 And there followed another angel, saying, Babylon is fallen, is fallen, that great city, because she made all nations drink of the wine of the wrath of her fornication.

They came together.

They preached brotherly love and tolerance.

They left out Jesus.

They left out the one person who can do these things.

They erred in their ways.

They paid a terrible price

~~~~~~~~~~~

Spiritual Thoughts

Doomed

The multitudes are in the valley of despair.

They were warned that God would judge them

They have drunk the wine of self.

They have served other Gods.

They are now reaping their misdeeds.

They are proud, and do not see the truth.

I weep for those who can not see.

I continually pray for them.

I counsel them to seek God.

They must make their choice.

They have no future without seeking His salvation.

They are lost without His grace.

~~~~~~~~~~~~~~~

The Shepard

The flocks graze upon the hillside

Some of the sheep are white and some are black.

The Shepard calls for His sheep to graze in fertile pastures.

Only the white sheep bid His call,

For they know His voice and follow Him.

The black sheep wander into a valley filled with green grass,

But there are many dangers.

They choose the danger to the Shepard,

They have sealed their fate.

Some will be eaten by wolves.

Some will find a shortage of food & drink.

They will never find peace without the Shepard.

The black sheep can wash themselves

With the blood of the Shepard.

Then they too can be white.

They can then follow the Shepard

And find His mercy & grace.

They have a choice.

~~~~~~~~~~~~~~~~~

Grandchildren

We see them less often.

Their voices are most welcomed.

They play freely in our home

(Continued Next Page)

Spiritual Thoughts

We patiently answer their questions.

We let them play their games.

They are our joy.

We should have had them first.

~~~~~~~~~~~~

God's Earthly Glory

I stand on the mountain top,

And see all God's glory.

Miles of forest lay before me,

With pine trees reaching for the heavens.

They are a protection from the elements.

To all the small animals gathered beneath them,

They are His protection for smaller creatures.

I see a vast ocean reaching unto the horizon.

It laps at the shore line of a peaceful town.

It has beneath its waves

Many unique and wondrous sea creatures.

It feeds the tiniest shrimp and the largest whale.

It can be frightening and it can be peaceful.

It can show forth God's love and His wrath.

God's glory abounds in the many things I see:

The beauty of the still lake.

The majesty of the oak tree.

The animals which He provides for.

The beauty of His wild flowers.

The beauty of His trees.

The soft clouds which drift by in a blue sky.

With all the beauty God provides,

Let us gaze with wonder and delight,

And forget the ugliness that man has made.

Let your eyes feast the beauty,

Let your senses smell His sweet delight,

Let your cares be given unto His loving arms.

Be at peace, for He is with you always.

~~~~~~~~~~~~~~~~~~~~

Sequencing

Matt. 13:30 Let both grow together until the harvest: and in the time of harvest I will say to the reapers, Gather ye together first the tares, and bind them in bundles to burn them: but gather the wheat into my barn.

(Continued Next Page)

Spiritual Thoughts

Rev 14:14-19

14 And I looked, and behold a white cloud, and upon the cloud *one* sat like unto the Son of man, having on his head a golden crown, and in his hand a sharp sickle.

15 And another angel came out of the temple, crying with a loud voice to him that sat on the cloud, Thrust in thy sickle, and reap: for the time is come for thee to reap; for the harvest of the earth is ripe.

16 And he that sat on the cloud thrust in his sickle on the earth; and the earth was reaped.

17 And another angel came out of the temple which is in heaven, he also having a sharp sickle.

18 And another angel came out from the altar, which had power over fire; and cried with a loud cry to him that had the sharp sickle, saying, Thrust in thy sharp sickle, and gather the clusters of the vine of the earth; for her grapes are fully ripe.

19 And the angel thrust in his sickle into the earth, and gathered the vine of the earth, and cast *it* into the great winepress of the wrath of God.

In Matthew we find the tares being thrust into the fire before the wheat is gathered into the barn.

In Revelation the good are reaped before the wicked.

Conflict? No! I believe as Jesus didn't know the time of these events, perhaps He didn't know of the order of these events.

Does it really matter or are these small things in the whole scheme of events? Rather than worry about the sequencing, we should keep our minds on the real purpose of our earthly existence - to bring others to Christ. The whys and wherefores will one day be revealed.

Let us commit ourselves to the present and the work set before us.

~~~~~~~~~~~~~~~~~~~~

Seeking God's Will Through Prayer

Set aside time each day. Don't allow things to be ahead of this time.

Read His Word unhurriedly. Let His Word become part of your heart.

Mark scripture as God reveals a meaning through it.

Mediate after reading in order to be in touch with God while in His throne room.

Do not ask for things for yourself, but praise and talk to Him as the spirit leads.

Pray for others and ask His will be done, He already knows your need before you ask.

You will find His will for your life.

You will receive His gifts without asking.

~~~~~~~~~~~~~~~~~~~~

A Warning

They seem to have all the answers.

They seem to be able to understand the hidden.

They seem to be able to discern all knowledge.

They are sure they are right & you are wrong.

Beware that you become not as they,

But according to God's knowledge imparted to you

(Continued Next Page)

Spiritual Thoughts

Seek His answers, not theirs.

Seek His unfailing wisdom.

~~~~~~~~~~~~~~~~~~~~~

My God is Like the Rose

I sit in solitude under the shade of a large maple.

The freshly cut grass is pleasant to my senses.

The breeze blows softly and often feels cool.

The sun warms me when I move into its light.

I see a garden before me.

In the midst a large rose beckons.

As I approach it opens wide to allow me to walk in its center.

It closes and I feel warmth and safety.

My God is like the rose.

Within His arms I feel safe.

His love is ever present.

His guidance sure.

Who is like my God?

Who can stretch forth his hand to ease hunger?

Who can cure all the ugliness of the land?

Who comforts during extreme darkness?

My God is all powerful.

My God created you and me.

My God waits to ease your pain.

My God loves all of His creation.

~~~~~~~~~~~~~

Working for God

I work for God now.

The pay is better!

~~~~~~~~~~~~~~~~~~~~

The Reunion

It was a joy to see them again.

We had parted tearfully many years before.

They had gone to the land where pain & suffering can not go.

They had exchanged their earthly raiment for robes of white.

We ate at the feast of the lamb.

We sang and gave praise to our creator.

(Continued Next Page)

Spiritual Thoughts

Our many questions were at last answered.

We knew eternity would be a blessing forever.

There were many stories of persecution.

There were many victory stories as well.

There was peace in our hearts.

He wiped away our tears and gave us joy.

(Continued Next Page)

How we long to meet our loved ones once again.

It will be a blessed event.

We shall have the answers for all our theological questions.

Our tribulations shall at last be over.

~~~~~~~~~~~~~

Know your enemy.

He is crafty.

He doesn't like to be thwarted.

He will fight back.

If you do good to a person who is hurting, look out!

God will protect you, but trial & tribulation is just around the corner.

God will use it for a test.

You can use it for a victory.

You can over come the enemy, for your God is much greater than he.

~~~~~~~~~~

Problem solving in the church

Mat 18:15-17

15 Moreover if thy brother shall trespass against thee, go and tell him his fault between thee and him alone: if he shall hear thee, thou hast gained thy brother.

16 But if he will not hear *thee, then* take with thee one or two more, that in the mouth of two or three witnesses every word may be established.

17 And if he shall neglect to hear them, tell *it* unto the church: but if he neglect to hear the church, let him be unto thee as a heathen man and a publican.

~~~~~~~~~~~~~~~~~~~~~

His day

He rises early.

He does his domestic chores.

He fills his body with the abundance of God.

He reads God's Word.

He mediates & prays.

He takes long walks in order to listen for God's voice.

He returns to his domicile to jot down the inspiration he was given.

His morning is filled with serving his family and his God.

After the noon meal he resumes his work for God.

He writes letters to his brethren to encourage.

He studies and makes notes to help spread the gospel.

He relaxes in the sound of heavenly singing.

(Continued Next Page)

Spiritual Thoughts

At evening his mate joins him from her labors in the town.

They give thanks and partake of God's abundance.

They spend a quiet time enjoying God's word & in prayer.

They counsel one another and share in the victories of the day.

There is little excitement in such a day.

Yet there is much joy in serving God.

There is joy in the success of the brethren.

There is much peace in the heart knowing He is with us.

~~~~~~~~~~~

He Is Risen!

If Jesus rose from the grave and transcended death, what have we to fear?

The victory is ours and nothing can hurt us for we will also transcend this earthly life.

Victorious we shall be in all our endeavors because He lives!

~~~~~~~~~

A Scary World

They are seeding the clouds with poisons.

They are spreading disease to weed out the weak.

They are subverting the powers that keep us free.

They are building Gulags for those who will not conform.

They are spreading lies & deceptions.

They are weakening the moral fabric or our society.

Does anyone remember Daniel & the lions or Shadrach, Meshach, & Abednego & the fiery furnace? We still serve a most powerful God.

~~~~~~~~~~~~~~~~~~~~

A Brother

He came to my door bearing gifts.

He also brought fear, pride, and bitterness.

He talked of things not advancing the Kingdom of God.

He had within, a great ability to teach.

I listened.

I prayed with and for him.

I counseled and ate at his table.

I tried to persuade him to abandon the cares of this world.

He became a burden. And quenched my spirit.

He called to say he was ill.

I had unchristian thoughts.

I shifted all my mercy away from him.

(Continued Next Page)

Spiritual Thoughts

In quiet solitude, I realized my sin.

I called a sister to help my brother.

I then asked God for forgiveness of my sin.

The test was over and my life better for the experience.

~~~~~~~~~~~~~

Service to the King

Serving each day.

Asking nothing in return.

Caring nothing for this life.

Feeling anxious for the end.

Could the unbeliever understand?

Unless you know the peace, joy, and hope,

You can not know the feeling.

Service is the only life for me.

My King is kind.

My King is full of love.

My King is a joy to serve.

My King only asks for love in return.

My King protects His own.

My King serves me more than I serve Him.

My King is wise and wonderful.

My King serves His justice to all

I shall follow His steps as He leads.

I shall bow before Him in respect, love, and joy.

I serve my King daily for the things He has given me.

Not material, but the intangibles.

The day draws ever closer.

The day will come as a thief.

I long for that day.

I shall be singing in that day.

I shall rejoice in that day

When I shall meet my King in person.

I shall sing and praise my King.

His sacrifice for me was greater than my service to Him.

~~~~~~~~~~~~~~~~~~~

Spiritual Thoughts

Have You . . .

Have you seen His power?

Have you seen Him heal?

Have you seen Him answer prayer?

Have you seen His eyes in the face of another?

Have you felt His presence?

Have you felt the power of His Word?

Have you felt His love?

Have you felt His protecting arms around you?

Did He give you words to say when they escaped you?

Did He give you strength to finish the task?

Did He lead you out of a dark place?

Do you know my Jesus?

~~~~~~~~~~~~~~~

Unchristian Behavior

Asking for forgiveness for the same thing over and over,

Is that repentance or willful disobedience?

~~~~~~~~~~~~~~~~~~~~~~~

Because of Him!

He was a part of the world, yet overcame it.

The victory is ours because of Him.

~~~~~~~~~~~~~~~~~~~~

Little Sins

Adam laying blame on Eve.

Noah drunk on wine.

Moses striking the rock in anger.

Peter's rebuke when thinking of self.

Even God's chosen made errors.

The problem is not correcting them.

Repentance means admitting your errors to God,

And as Jesus said, "Sin no more."

As you rid yourself of small sins,

The challenges come in larger portions.

As you meet each challenge,

Remember God is there to help you.

(Continued Next Page)

Spiritual Thoughts

Each victory over Satan and sin

Makes us stronger for the next challenge.

As we grow, the smaller challenges

Become easier to over come.

Grow in strength.

Grow in power to overcome.

Grow in grace.

Grow in maturity.

Our heavenly Father is watching.

He is listening.

He is helping.

Our heavenly Father wants us to succeed.

~~~~~~~~~~~~~

God's Children

The wayward woman

The disobedient child

The lawless man

The corrupt official

All will find justice.

All can find rest.

All can seek salvation.

For God wants all to repent and be baptized into Christ.

~~~~~~~~~~~~~~~~~~~~

The Voice

Their buildings lay in ruins.

Their proudest achievements were brought low.

Misery and desolation lay before them.

They cried to heaven, "Why have you forgotten us?"

From heaven was heard,

I have not forgotten you,

You have forgotten me.

You built a great nation based on my laws.

You founded many churches in my name.

You spread the gospel to many nations.

Your form of government was scattered upon the earth.

At the height of your greatness you began to abandon my laws.

My justice you took out of your legal system.

(Continued Next Page)

Spiritual Thoughts

You took me out of your schools.

You allowed fornications and depravities into your society.

You took me off your money.

You replaced my goodness with greed.

You puffed yourselves up beyond your abilities.

You took out the corner stone from your daily lives.

Many of your churches preach man's beliefs, not mine.

They allow you to worship graven images.

They allow tolerance for things not in scripture.

They water down the truth.

You have turned your back on the Creator.

Your pride, greed, and ignorance have brought you here.

I loved you, but you rejected me.

You now reap the harvest that you have sown.

~~~~~~~~~~~~~~~~

Church Marquee

If God is your co-pilot,

Change seats.

~~~~~~~~~~~~~~~~~~

Little Voices

Little voices that never sang.

Little voices that never cried.

Little voices that were never gently held.

Little voices that never had a choice.

Mothers who weep for little voices never born.

Mothers who wonder about little voices never born

Mothers trying to forget little voices never born.

Mothers who are indifferent to little voices never born.

Little voices are still loved,

By a creator who now holds them.

Little voices will one day

See their mothers stand at judgment.

Little voices we weep for you.

~~~~~~~~~~~~~~~~~~~

Isaiah 44:2 This is what the Lord says- he who made you, who formed you in the womb, and who will help you: Do not be afraid

~~~~~~~~~~~~~~

Spiritual Thoughts

Satan's Walls

Whenever Satan places a wall in your path,

God either gives you a map to get around it

Or a ladder to get over it.

~~~~~~~~~~

Conspiracy Theories

He speaks of them poisoning us.

He speaks of gulags being built to hold us.

He speaks of reducing our numbers by disease.

He speaks of the deception of their words.

He is very sure of his knowledge.

I ask if he has a solution.

He does not answer.

Luckily, we have a God who does.

~~~~~~~~~~~~~~~~

Moment by Moment
By Doris E.

Happy moments - praise God.

Difficult moments - seek God.

Quiet moments - worship God.

Painful moments - trust God.

Every moment - thank God.

~~~~~~~~~~~~~

Community Gossip

Some thought her odd.

Some talked of her quirks.

Some talked of her misdeeds.

Some pitied her.

Some speculated, only God knew the truth.

~~~~~~~~~~~~~

From Darkness

In darkness He sought me,

And brought me through His Word into the light.

He breathed on me His Spirit,

And dwelt within me.

His Spirit continues to direct me,

As onward I let Him lead.

His Spirit searches my heart

And brings to the light the sin sometimes found there.

(Continued Next Page)

Spiritual Thoughts

When I confess every sin brought to mind

I am relieved of yet one more tie to this world.

I am closer to being Christ-like

A state which I long for.

In darkness we dwell

Until He comes and shines forth His light.

We dare not miss the chance

For eternity is a long time to be without hope.

~~~~~~~~~~~~~~~

Romans Eight

If God be for us, who can stand against us?

Nothing in heaven or on earth shall separate us from the love of God, we have in Christ Jesus

~~~~~~~~~~~~~~~~~~~~

Children of Many Shades

Children of darkness find only self.

They find pleasure in the world

They seek satisfaction in things.

They see life as ending at death.

Children of gray seek the middle ground.

They have found salvation, and seek no more.

They hide their light lest others may see.

They wait for eternity, but seek not another to take with them.

Children of light see the future.

They seek to share the gospel with all.

They are not afraid of what the world thinks of them.

They have found grace and hope.

What shade are you?

If you know Jesus, praise God!

Share your light that God's kingdom can grow.

Be not afraid, for God will help you spread this message.

~~~~~~~~~~~~~~~~

Misinformed

They learn tolerance.

They learn of Your love.

They learn of Your mighty deeds.

They never learn of Your hatred for sin.

(Continued Next Page)

Spiritual Thoughts

Some feel You made the world

Then let man choose his own destiny.

They say we need to take care of ourselves,

For You have abandoned us.

Then there are those who feel You don't exist.

All have found man's meaning for life.

None have read the scriptures.

The end will come suddenly for them.

God's word will stand forever.

His Word must be read and spread.

The Way is clear.

We all must follow Jesus.

~~~~~~~~~~~~~~~~~~~~

2 Thessalonians 2:1

. . . God will send them strong delusion, that they should believe a lie:

~~~~~~~~~~~~~~

Items of Antiquity

The ark of the Ten Commandments

The ark that brought Noah over the flood

The cross which bore our Savior

The Holy Grail

If I need to see these things, where is my faith?

~~~~~~~~~~~~~~~~~~~~

2Corinthians 5:7
(For we walk by faith, not by sight :)
~~~~~~~~~~~~~~

Unfinished

A person you didn't have time to tell about Jesus

Increasing your prayer or scripture reading

Unconfessed sin

Asking a brother for forgiveness

Spending more time on affairs of the Kingdom

Seeking to be more like the master

~~~~~~~~~~~~~~~~~~~~

Revelation 22:20
. . . (Jesus) "Surely I come quickly." Amen. Even so, come, Lord Jesus.
~~~~~~~~~~~~~~~~~

Spiritual Thoughts

A Narrow Road

The broad way beckons to a people not in tune with God.

They are ignorant of His Word.

They listen to a watered down truth.

They believe what they have heard but do not research the truth.

The heart is the key to obeying God

For God knows what is in your heart.

It is not enough to do what is right before men

It is necessary to do what is right in secret.

God is a merciful God

God is a gracious God

God is a just God.

God is a God who hates sin.

You can not be a child of His

Unless you accept Christ & be baptized.

There is only one walk after this

The continuing examining of the heart for sin.

We serve a jealous God.

We need to put Him first

We need to obey His commands

We need to love Him as He loves us.

Thru continuous improvement we become Christ-like

But only if we get rid of self.

We must not worry about material things

We can't take them to our final destination.

We walk a narrow road.

We are pilgrims in a world that sees us as strange.

We follow a person who will never let us down.

We follow the Truth, the Life, & the Way.

~~~~~~~~~~~~~~~

Matthew 7:13

Enter ye in at the strait gate: for wide *is* the gate, and broad *is* the way, that leadeth to destruction, and many there be which go in thereat: (Jesus)

~~~~~~~~~~~~~~~~~~~~~

Spiritual Thoughts

Enemy Harassment

She felt his presence.

He threatened to do her harm.

He told her lies.

She felt depressed.

Many times she was in this situation.

Many times she asked for help from her brothers and sisters.

She cried out to God and Jesus for help.

She was in torment and grief.

Her problem was one she had created.

She allowed anger and jealousy, into her heart.

She left the door open for him to come in.

She was unwilling to face the problem.

How better to admit to our failings.

Ask our brother or sister for forgiveness.

Ask God for forgiveness.

Seek to empty our heart for Jesus.

A heart emptied of anger, malicious, and other negative emotions

Allow God to fill it with joy, happiness, and other positive emotions.

Reduce the negative to increase the positive.

Live a happier life in Jesus.

~~~~~~~~~~~~~~~

The Tithe

Because it was for a love offering, I took it from my tithe.

Be cause it was for gospel records, I took it from my tithe.

Because it was a course that would help me spiritually, I took it from my tithe.

Because it was for helping out a family at church, I took it from my tithe.

Because it was for something I did for the church, I took it from my tithe.

Have you shortchanged God?

~~~~~~~~~~~~~~~~~~

2Cor. 8:12

For if there be first a willing mind, *it is* accepted according to that a man hath, *and* not according to that he hath not.

~~~~~~~~~~~~~

Spiritual Thoughts

A Small Start

It started small.

It grew larger and more numerous.

As it spread it destroyed much.

It destroyed friendships, marriages, lives.

It turned neighbors against each other.

It separated families.

It split churches.

It destroyed Christian witnessing.

It was only a small white lie.

It was sin and pride.

It was an abomination to God.

It could have been avoided.

Isn't truth a part of the armor of God?

~~~~~~~~~~~

What If?

What if you had a son?

What if you sent him away to do your will?

What if he were disobedient?

What if he decided that he could do whatever he pleased?

Thank you Jesus for doing the will of your Father.

~~~~~~~~~~~~~~

Look with Better Vision

See men as God does.

Look not at the outward appearance,

But look in the soul and heart.

Even though men have sin

God has a cure.

The gospel over comes the disease of sin.

~~~~~~~~~~~~~~~~

Romans 6:23

For the wages of sin is death, but the gift of God is eternal life through Jesus Christ our Lord.

~~~~~~~~~~~~~~~~~~~~

Study

Studying geology to better understand the earth.

Studying philosophy for an understanding of man.

Studying anatomy to finding a cure for diseases.

Studying political science to better understand government.

(Continued Next Page)

Spiritual Thoughts

All of these may be worthwhile to the common man.

Studying scripture is the only future we have.

The answers between Genesis and Revelation are our salvation.

The only important thing is our relationship with God.

~~~~~~~~~~~~~~~~~~

The Test

I was led into a room blindfolded.

I was seated at a table.

I was told to put my hand on the table, palm up.

Six people entered the room.

One at a time, each laid four fingers on my palm.

I then was led into another room.

With the blindfold then removed,

I was asked the race of each set of fingers.

To God all humans are transparent.

There is no color on the outside that God does not like.

God looks at hearts and souls.

God seeks those things mankind can't see.

If we trace back to our ancestors,

We finally come to Adam and Eve.

If we are all descended from the same two people,

How can there be racial hatred?

Let us see things the way God does.

Let us be Christ-like in our feelings toward others.

Let us love each other, as Christ loved us.

Let us see each other in the light of love.

~~~~~~~~~~~~~~~~~

Mark 12:30-31

30 And thou shalt love the Lord thy God with all thy heart, and with all thy soul, and with all thy mind, and with all thy strength: this *is* the first commandment.

31 And the second *is* like, *namely* this, Thou shalt love thy neighbor as thyself. There is none other commandment greater than these.

~~~~~~~~~~~~~~~~~~~~

Praise God, Praise Jesus

Jesus came down from Glory.

He took the form of man.

Jesus suffered and died.

He overcame death on the third day.

(Continued Next Page)

Spiritual Thoughts

Jesus sits on the right side of His Father.

He intercedes for us.

Jesus bestows on us the gift of the Holy Spirit.

He gives us other spiritual gifts as well.

God is an awesome deity.

He created all the heavens and the earth.

God does wondrous things.

He parted the waters for Moses to pass.

God heals the sick.

He protects His own.

God has a great love for His creations.

He sent Jesus to redeem them.

Should we then trust in another or ourselves?

Should we try to redeem ourselves?

We may think there is a way that is more perfect than God's,

But we fool ourselves, and condemn ourselves.

God is an awesome god.

His power is beyond the imaginations of men.

God knows our past and our future.

His relationship with man will be accomplished as He predicted.

~~~~~~~~~~~~~~~~~~~~~~~~~~~~~~~

2Chronicles 7:13-15

13 If I shut up heaven that there be no rain, or if I command the locusts to devour the land, or if I send pestilence among my people;

14 If my people, which are called by my name, shall humble themselves, and pray, and seek my face, and turn from their wicked ways; then will I hear from heaven, and will forgive their sin, and will heal their land.

15 Now mine eyes shall be open, and mine ears attent unto the prayer [that is made] in this place.

~~~~~~~~~~~~~~~~~

Romans 9:33

... Behold, I lay in Zion a stumbling stone and a rock of offense: and whosoever believeth on him shall not be ashamed.

~~~~~~~~~~~~~~~~~~~~

I Gave My Life for Thee
Havergal/ Bliss

I gave my life for thee, My precious blood I shed

That thou may ransomed be, And quickened from the dead;

I gave My life for thee - What hast thou given for me?

(Continued Next Page)

Spiritual Thoughts

My Father's house of light, My glory circled throne

I left, for earthly night, For wanderings sad and lone;

I left it all for thee - Hast thou left aught for me?

I suffered much for thee, More than thy tongue can tell,

Of bittrest agony, to rescue thee from hell;

I've borne it all for thee - What hast thou borne for me?

And I have brought to thee, Down from my home above.

Salvation full and free, My pardon and My love;

I bring rich gifts to thee - What hast thou brought to me?

~~~~~~~~~~~~~~~~~~~

Suddenly It Happened

It was an average blue sky day when the clouds rolled in.

It was to be a terrible and joyful day.

Some would be excited and joyful.

Many would be trembling and fearful

All work was put aside.

Transportation was at a standstill.

There was no cursing to be heard.

There was a loud silence.

Finally, persecution was stopped.

At long last, the truth could overcome.

Satan's lies were destroyed in an instant.

The King had come to claim His bride.

~~~~~~~~~~~~~~~~~~~~

Rev 22:20
He which testifieth these things saith, Surely I come quickly. Amen
Even so, come, Lord Jesus.

~~~~~~~~~~~~~~~~

At Mom's Passing

From a coma, she opened her eyes.

She looked into the face of her Creator.

She snuggled herself into His arms.

She closed her eyes.

Her breathing became easier.

She took her last breath.

(Continued Next Page)

Spiritual Thoughts

There were tears from all who loved her.

But tears soon calmed our souls.

She had left to be with Jesus.

But we knew we would one day see her again.

For God's son had a victory

Where as now, because of Him, it gives us hope.

We have memories of times past.

We have comfort from friends and family.

We can always remember;

When we gathered at her bedside and read scriptures,

When we told her we loved her for the last time.

When we prayed for God's will to be done.

She has left her body to be with Jesus.

No more will she see pain or sorrow.

She looks over us now from heaven above.

And is comforted by His great love.

Soon we shall all be together,

When our earthly work is done.

I look forward to seeing her again.

To meeting all those loved ones who have gone on before.

Mom will be there to welcome me home.

She will show me heaven's glory.

She will introduce me to our Savior,

The One who made it all possible.

~~~~~~~~~~~~~~~~~~~

1Thessalonians 4:13-14

13 But I would not have you to be ignorant, brethren, concerning them which are asleep, that ye sorrow not, even as others which have no hope.

14 For if we believe that Jesus died and rose again, even so them also which sleeps in Jesus will God bring with him.

~~~~~~~~~~~~~~~~~~~~

One Special Night

There was no room in the inn,

So a stable was where He was born.

Humble beginnings for one so great.

Small in size, great in power.

Three wise men came bearing gifts.

Angels proclaimed His birth.

Shepherds came in wonder.

Angels watched over Him.

(Continued Next Page)

Spiritual Thoughts

His names were: Wonderful, Savior, Redeemer, Messiah,

Prince of Peace, Corner-Stone.

Elect of God, Glory of the Lord,

Lord of Lords, King of Kings.

Praise be to God for this blessed event!

Praise be to God for our salvation!

Praise be to God for our example!

Praise be to God for The Way!

~~~~~~~~~~~~~~~~~~~~~

Luke 2:7-16

7 And she brought forth her firstborn son, and wrapped him in swaddling clothes, and laid him in a manger; because there was no room for them in the inn.

8 And there were in the same country shepherds abiding in the field, keeping watch over their flock by night.

9 And, lo, the angel of the Lord came upon them, and the glory of the Lord shone round about them: and they were sore afraid.

10 And the angel said unto them, Fear not: for, behold, I bring you good tidings of great joy, which shall be to all people.

11 For unto you is born this day in the city of David a Savior, which is Christ the Lord.

12 And this *shall be* a sign unto you; Ye shall find the babe wrapped in swaddling clothes, lying in a manger.

13 And suddenly there was with the angel a multitude of the heavenly host praising God, and saying,

14 Glory to God in the highest, and on earth peace, good will toward men.

15 And it came to pass, as the angels were gone away from them into heaven, the shepherds said one to another, Let us now go even unto Bethlehem, and see this thing which is come to pass, which the Lord hath made known unto us.

16 And they came with haste, and found Mary, and Joseph, and the babe lying in a manger.

~~~~~~~~~~~~~~~~~~~~~

A Church for a New Age

Our building is new.

It is large because of the number of our church members.

It is very modern.

Each spring, a florist puts in our flowers.

Inside, the pews have cushions for our flock.

The music is upbeat, with a touch of rock.

The singing is traditional, but lively.

It sets the stage for the service.

Our pastor is young.

He knows the bible well.

He preaches about a god of love.

He'd like the whole world to come together.

(Continued Next Page)

Spiritual Thoughts

You will not learn of the wrath of God.

You will not learn of Satan and hell.

You will not learn the full gospel.

You will see happy, smiling faces.

Our church has social events.

We all like to go to the picnics,

To the concerts during the week.

The concerts allow us to see secular bands.

Attendance is getting better.

The singing more joyful,

The preaching softer.

We are becoming more accepted of the world.

~~~~~~~~~~~~~~~~~~~~

2Corinthians 6:17

Wherefore come out from among them, and be ye separate, saith the Lord, and touch not the unclean *thing*, and I will receive you.

~~~~~~~~~~~~

Acts 2:40

And with many other words did he testify and exhort, saying, Save yourselves from this perverse generation.

~~~~~~~~~~~~~~~~~~~~~

Finishing God's Plan

Solomon built God's House in the city.

One day, God will bring our city into His House

~~~~~~~~~~~~~~~~~~

Like A Child

The B-I-B-L-E,

Yes, that's the book for me.

Jesus loves me! This I know,

For the Bible tells me so;

Little ones to Him to belong,

They are weak but He is strong.

God is so good to me.

Love Him in the morning,

Remember He loves you.

He's got the whole world in His hands.

I'm in the Lord's army.

(Continued Next Page)

Spiritual Thoughts

This little light, I'm goin' let it shine.

Trust and obey,

For it's the only way,

To be happy in Jesus.

Whisper a prayer at morning - evening - noon.

Jesus may come in the morning - evening - noon

So keep your heart in tune.

O be careful little hands what you do

O be careful little mouth what you say.

O be careful little eyes what you see.

O be careful little feet where you go.

~~~~~~~~~~~~~~~~~~~~

Matt. 18:3

. . . Verily I say unto you, Except ye be converted, and become as little children, ye shall not enter into the kingdom of heaven.

~~~~~~~~~~~~~~~~~~~~

Storms

C. Nobel

Storms may come,

And storms may go,

But Jesus is always there.

~~~~~~~~~~~~~~

Angels

He may be on a street corner begging for food.

He may be someone you gave a ride.

~~~~~~~~~~~~~~~~~~~~

Heb 13:2

Be not forgetful to entertain strangers: for thereby some have entertained angels unawares.

~~~~~~~~~~~~~~~~

Variety

God made so many colors of people.

God has allowed a few different paths on the Narrow Way.

There are many different intensities of worship.

There is only one Way to Eternity with Christ.

~~~~~~~~~~~~~~~~~~~~~~~~

Spiritual Thoughts

Our Witness

A magazine or a book, a record or a tape;

A collectable or a mug, a picture or a trophy;

A word from our mouth, a place that we go;

Non Christian people we like to be with.

What is ruining your witness?

~~~~~~~~~~~~~~~~~~~~

2Corinthians 5:17

Therefore if any man *be* in Christ, *he is* a new creature: old things are passed away; behold, all things are become new.

Colossians 3:10

And have put on the new *man,* which is renewed in knowledge after the image of him that created him:

~~~~~~~~~~~~~~~~~~~~

Thank you, Lord

When mortars fell and took other men,

You saved me.

When bullets flew and others died,

You saved me.

In the hospital, my organs failed to function,

You turned them back on.

In the emergency room, they told my wife to call my closest kin,

You brought me back from the brink.

When ever I needed you,

You were there.

Even when I didn't call for you,

You were there.

The beginning of wisdom,

Is realization of the workings of God.

Even when we don't call on Him,

He knows we are His, and delivers us.

He is far more faithful to us,

Than we are to Him.

His greatness can not be measured.

His grace is more beautiful the more we grow.

Thank you for trials and tribulations

This strengthens me.

(Continued Next Page)

Spiritual Thoughts

Thank you for chastisement,

This makes me a better man.

Thank you for the Holy Spirit,

This teaches and spurs me on.

Thank you for Jesus,

Whose sufferings helped to cleanse my sins.

Thank you for creating me in your image,

Which makes me to try to live up to your expectations.

Thank you for your love

That is everlasting.

~~~~~~~~~~~~~~~~~~~~

Revival Needed

Abortions, immorality, gambling;

Deceit, gay marriage, the occult.

The evil surrounds us,

But we shall not cease praying for deliverance.

We need a turning back to our God.

We need a turning back to conservative values.

We need a nation on its knees.

We need a revival.

From the Old Testament we find God dealing with sin.

He destroyed nations for idolatry.

He destroyed Sodom and Gomorrah for immorality.

He punished Israel for turning away from Him.

~~~~~~~~~~~~~~~~~~~~

Romans 2:8-9

But unto them that are contentious, and do not obey the truth, but obey unrighteousness, indignation and wrath,

Tribulation and anguish, upon every soul of man that doeth evil, of the Jew first, and also of the Gentile;

Ephesians 5:5-6

5 For this ye know, that no whoremonger, nor unclean person, nor covetous man, who is an idolater, hath any inheritance in the kingdom of Christ and of God.

6 Let no man deceive you with vain words: for because of these things cometh the wrath of God upon the children of disobedience.

~~~~~~~~~~~~~~~~~~~~~~~~~~~~

Prayer

Quantity with little substance

Or quality with earnest talk.

(Continued Next Page)

Spiritual Thoughts

Remember, prayer is talking directly to

the Creator of All Things.

~~~~~~~~~~~~~~~~~~~~~

Matthew 6:7-8

7 But when ye pray, use not vain repetitions, as the heathen *do*: for they think that they shall be heard for their much speaking.

8 Be not ye therefore like unto them: for your Father knoweth what things ye have need of, before ye ask him.   (Jesus)

~~~~~~~~~~~~~~~~~~~~~

Humility - Not Hypocrisy

We come to church to worship,

Not for a fashion show.

We ask our brothers and sisters of their situation,

Not for gossip.

We sing the hymns to praise God,

Not to show our pride in harmony.

We listen to the sermon, searching our heart for uncleanliness,

Not to accuse others.

We ask for forgiveness for sins we plan to avoid with God's help,

Not, so we can do them again.

We seek God's direction in our lives,

Not our own.

We pray and study scripture daily,

Not once a week.

We seek God's wisdom and strength,

Not the world's.

We humble ourselves before God,

For pride has left us.

We look at situations and praise God,

Not give anyone or thing the credit, but Him.

We seek God's acceptance,

For we are His.

~~~~~~~~~~~~~~~~~~~~

Matthew 23:27-28

27 Woe unto you, scribes and Pharisees, hypocrites! for ye are like unto whited sepulchers, which indeed appear beautiful outward, but are within full of dead *men's* bones, and of all uncleanness.

28 Even so ye also outwardly appear righteous unto men, but within ye are full of hypocrisy and iniquity. (Jesus)

~~~~~~~~~~~~~~~~~~~~~~~

The Keys

A Bible Believing Church

Studying God's Word

(Continued Next Page)

Spiritual Thoughts

Accepting Christ

Being Baptized

Prayer

Seeking wisdom

Witnessing to bring others to Christ

Living Christ-like

Casting off self, pride, ego

~~~~~~~~~~~~~~~~~~~~

My Rock and Fortress

When troubles come,

And the wind and rain beat upon myself,

I shall not hide,

For Jesus is there with me.

He will protect me from all that comes.

He never leaves in time of trouble.

He only waits for me to call.

He shields me from all the arrows of my enemy.

In Jesus I can trust.

Friends come and go,

But He is always there,

For He is my constant friend and companion.

If you need someone to be beside you.

To fight your daily woes.

There is no greater friend than Jesus,

Of this, you will come to know.

~~~~~~~~~~~~~~~~~~~~

The Bible - Our Sword

The Word of God	**Written with a purpose**
Despised by the foolish	To authenticate the divinity of Christ
The Book of the Ages	To give hope to men
Food for the Soul	To relate human experience as a warning
Divinely inspired	To give knowledge of eternal life
Precepts written in the heart	Furnishes a light
Loved by the saints	Absolutely trustworthy
Mighty in its influence	Profitable for instruction
A blessing to those who reverence	Perilous to the ignorant
Purifies the life	Contains the commandments of God
Contains seed -corn for the sower	A devouring flame, A crushing hammer,
The standard of faith and duty	A life giving force, A saving power,
Its words sacred	A defensive weapon, A probing instrument

~~~~~~~~~~~~~~~~~~~~

Spiritual Thoughts

Psalms 31:3

For thou *art* my rock and my fortress; therefore for thy name's sake lead me, and guide me.

~~~~~~~~~~~~~~~~~~~

Investments

God has invested...

Your life

His Son's death upon the cross

His words for you to learn

His daily blessings.

Have you invested in Him?

~~~~~~~~~~~~~~~~

God is my strength

I rest in His shadow.

All I do, I do for Him.

He is my strength and all my wisdom.

He is my salvation.

When I try to do things without Him, I fail.

My ideas lack His wisdom.

When I try to fight this world's evil,

Without Him I fail.

If I set aside self and pride, and allow God to intervene,

Then He works to free me from my woes.

Things of this world may have beauty,

But God's beauty and power far outdistance them.

Who can rest in his own works,

And expect to reap heavenly rewards?

Who can fashion his own salvation,

And expect to rest in eternity?

There is only one God.

There is only one Way.

There is only one Gospel.

There is only one road to eternity.

~~~~~~~~~~~~~~~~~~~

Proverbs 2:5-7

5 Then shalt thou understand the fear of the LORD, and find the knowledge of God.

6 For the LORD giveth wisdom: out of his mouth *cometh* knowledge and understanding.

7 He layeth up sound wisdom for the righteous: *he is* a shield to them that walk uprightly.

~~~~~~~~~~~~~~~~~~~

Spiritual Thoughts

The Sinful Nature

I was in darkness but He found me.

I found salvation.

I rejoiced at baptism.

I begin studying scripture.

I soaked up knowledge of God from many sources.

I witnessed to my family and friends.

I handed out tracts at every opportunity.

I prayed daily for others.

Months grew into years,

Expectations grew into doubt,

Doubt grew into self serving,

Self serving grew into sin.

Satan is long on patience.

The Prince of Darkness uses time

And situations to trap us,

Or diversions to lead us away from God.

God is long on patience.

The Master of Light uses scripture

To bring us back to Him

Through prayer and repentance.

Take heed that you always keep in check

Your pride, self, lust, and other sins of the flesh.

God will forgive sin and your nature

But He expects us to keep up our guard.

~~~~~~~~~~~~~~~~~~~

Ephesians 5:2-5
2 And walk in love, as Christ also hath loved us, and hath given himself for us an offering and a sacrifice to God for a sweet smelling savor.
3 But fornication, and all uncleanness, or covetousness, let it not be once named among you, as becometh saints;
4 Neither filthiness, nor foolish talking, nor jesting, which are not convenient: but rather giving of thanks.
5 For this ye know, that no whoremonger, nor unclean person, nor covetous man, who is an idolater, hath any inheritance in the kingdom of Christ and of God.

1John 2:15-17
15 Love not the world, neither the things *that are* in the world. If any man love the world, the love of the Father is not in him.
16 For all that *is* in the world, the lust of the flesh, and the lust of the eyes, and the pride of life, is not of the Father, but is of the world.
17 And the world passeth away, and the lust thereof: but he that doeth the will of God abideth forever.

(Continued Next Page)

Spiritual Thoughts

1Thessalonians 5:8-23

8 But let us, who are of the day, be sober, putting on the breastplate of faith and love; and for a helmet, the hope of salvation.

9 For God hath not appointed us to wrath, but to obtain salvation by our Lord Jesus Christ,

10 Who died for us, that, whether we wake or sleep, we should live together with him.

11 Wherefore comfort yourselves together, and edify one another, even as also ye do.

12 And we beseech you, brethren, to know them which labor among you, and are over you in the Lord, and admonish you;

13 And to esteem them very highly in love for their work's sake. *And* be at peace among yourselves.

14 Now we exhort you, brethren, warn them that are unruly, comfort the feebleminded, support the weak, be patient toward all *men*.

15 See that none render evil for evil unto any *man*; but ever follow that which is good, both among yourselves, and to all *men*.

16 Rejoice evermore.

17 Pray without ceasing.

18 In every thing give thanks: for this is the will of God in Christ Jesus concerning you.

19 Quench not the Spirit.

20 Despise not prophesying.

21 Prove all things; hold fast that which s good.

22 Abstain from all appearance of evil.

23 And the very God of peace sanctify you wholly; and *I pray God* your whole spirit and soul and body be preserved blameless unto the coming of our Lord Jesus Christ.

Matthew 15:18-20 (Jesus)

18 . . . those things which proceed out of the mouth come forth from the heart; and they defile the man.

19 For out of the heart proceed evil thoughts, murders, adulteries, fornications, thefts, false witness, and blasphemies:

20 These are *the things* which defile a man. . .

~~~~~~~~~~~~~~~~~~~~~~~~~~

Ignorance and Attitude

I chose not to believe in God,

For when I asked Him

To take relieve me of my situation,

Nothing happened.

Of course, I hadn't taken the time to accept Jesus.

I haven't really sought His help with humility.

I want Him to help me,

But I don't want to serve Him.

I want Him to be a part of my life without obligation.

I want my situation to change without me changing.

This whole belief thing is not geared toward me.

I want God to do my bidding.

I don't want to read or understand scripture,

Or go to church, or pray daily,

Or humble myself before God

I am too busy.

(Continued Next Page)

Spiritual Thoughts

I'll just go on my way,

Doing my own thing.

There is nothing to fear in this world

For I know the present is all there is.

~~~~~~~~~~~~~~~~~~~~

2Peter 3:9-14

9 The Lord is not slack concerning his promise, as some men count slackness; but is longsuffering to us-ward, not willing that any should perish, but that all should come to repentance.

10 But the day of the Lord will come as a thief in the night; in which the heavens shall pass away with a great noise, and the elements shall melt with fervent heat, the earth also and the works that are therein shall be burned up.

11 Seeing then *that* all these things shall be dissolved, what manner *of persons* ought ye to be in *all* holy conversation and godliness,

12 Looking for and hasting unto the coming of the day of God, wherein the heavens being on fire shall be dissolved, and the elements shall melt with fervent heat?

13 Nevertheless we, according to his promise, look for new heavens and a new earth, wherein dwelleth righteousness.

14 Wherefore, beloved, seeing that ye look for such things, be diligent that ye may be found of him in peace, without spot, and blameless.

~~~~~~~~~~~~~~~~~~~~

Reasonable Proof

The beating: Matt. 26:67, Matt. 27:26, Matt. 27:30

Professional executors proclaim Him dead: John 19:33, Mark 15:44-45

Earthquakes at His death: Matt. 27:54

The embalming: John 19:39-40

The rock blocking the tomb is moved: Mark 16:3-4

The guards? Matt 27:65-66, Acts 12:19

He frees Himself from the linen after death: Luke 24:12

He walks: John 20:25-27

~~~~~~~~~~~~~~~~~~~

Romans 6:8-9
Now if we be dead with Christ, we believe that we shall also live with him:
Knowing that Christ being raised from the dead dieth no more; death hath no more dominion over him.

~~~~~~~~~~~~~~~~

Because of Him!

I am saved.

I walk daily with Him.

I read His word.

I mediate on His word

I pray.

I seek righteousness.

I confess sins to keep my heart pure.

I confess Him to others.

I serve Him with willingness of heart

(Continued Next Page)

Spiritual Thoughts

I fear nothing.

I fear not death.

I have hope and peace.

I shall live eternally.

~~~~~~~~~~~~~~~~~~

Romans 8:38-39

38 For I am persuaded, that neither death, nor life, nor angels, nor principalities, nor powers, nor things present, nor things to come,

39 Nor height, nor depth, nor any other creature, shall be able to separate us from the love of God, which is in Christ Jesus our Lord.

~~~~~~~~~~~~~~~~~~

It All Adds Up

Knowledge of the Truth, plus;

Acceptance of Jesus plus;

Repentance of sin,

Equals;

Salvation, plus;

Relief of burdens, plus,

Peace of mind, plus;

Hope and joy, plus;

A new friend named Jesus, plus

Total access to God.

K,T+A,J+R,S = S+R,B+P,M+H+J+N,F,N,J+T,A,T,G

For just a little, you receive an abundance.

~~~~~~~~~~~~~~~~~~~~

The Bible

(444 Surprising Quotes about the Bible Bethany House Publishers)

The Bible without the Holy Spirit

Is a sundial by moonlight.

Dwight L. Moody

^^^^^^^^^^^^^^^^^^^^

The Scriptures should only be read in an attitude of prayer,

Trusting the inward working of the Holy Spirit

To make the truths a living reality within us.

William Law

^^^^^^^^^^^^^^^^^^^^

(Continued Next Page)

Spiritual Thoughts

It outlives, out lifts, out loves, out reaches,

Out ranks, out runs all other books.

Trust it, love it, obey it, and Eternal life is yours.

A.Z. Conrad

∧∧∧∧∧∧∧∧∧∧∧∧∧∧

Lay hold on the Bible

Until the Bible lays hold on you.

William H. Houghton

~~~~~~~~~~~~~~~~~~~~

Beware of False Doctrine

They came to my door talking about God.

They raised my awareness.

They offered materials for me to study.

They set a time to shortly return.

They returned the next week and entered my door.

They spoke about God and left much literature.

They came many more weeks and seemed so sincere.

They soon invited me to their church.

The building was low key, not fancy or grand.

They preached about God and read from their Bible.

I soon wanted my own Bible to read and to study.

I also wanted the book that teaches me to bring others in.

I believed their interpretations.

I never came to doubt.

I never searched for any other truth.

I believed theirs was the only way.

I now seek my truth in a different way.

I compare their beliefs to the true Word of God.

I study The Word by checking the Hebrew and the Greek.

I test all Man's saying with Scripture.

~~~~~~~~~~~~~~~~~~~

Matthew 7:15

Beware of false prophets, which come to you in sheep's clothing, but inwardly they are ravening wolves. (Jesus)

~~~~~~~~~~~~~~~~~

Spiritual Thoughts

Matthew 7:22-23

22 Many will say to me in that day, Lord, Lord, have we not prophesied in thy name and in thy name have cast out devils? And in thy name done many wonderful works?

23 And then will I profess unto them, I never knew you: depart from me, ye that work iniquity. (Jesus)

~~~~~~~~~~~~~~~~~~~~

Romans 10:16-17

16 But they have not all obeyed the gospel. For Isaiah saith, Lord, who hath believed our report?

17 So then faith *cometh* by hearing, and hearing by the word of God.

~~~~~~~~~~~~~~~~~~~~

Who Knows!

Is it a well kept secret?

Do your co-workers know?

Do friends and family know?

How about the store clerk down the street?

Is Jesus a companion you keep in secret?

Is your Christianity a known fact?

Is the gospel something you are willing to share?

When will you spread the Word?

~~~~~~~~~~~~~~~~~~~~

Romans 1:16

For I am not ashamed of the gospel of Christ: for it is the power of God unto salvation to every one that believeth; to the Jew first, and also to the Greek.

~~~~~~~~~~~~~~~~~~

Fear of the Future

For years they spread fear.

The Anti-Christ was everywhere and everyone.

The one world government was just around the corner.

Our rights were being taken away.

Does it really matter when these things will take place?

Is not the real question, are we ready?

Is not God still on the throne?

Is not our future to be with Him?

God will triumph over evil.

God's Word is the only truth we need.

The future has been written.

As Jesus overcame death and the world, so shall we!

(Continued Next Page)

Spiritual Thoughts

Fear not death or circumstances of this world.

Care not what the world calls you.

Pray for the unsaved that persecute you.

They are lost without Jesus.

Your future is guaranteed by Scripture.

You have only one fear.

The fear of not reaching as many as you can.

We have much work to do.

~~~~~~~~~~~~~~~~~~~

The Days of My Conversion

That morning I rose early.

My stomach was in distress.

The porcelain throne received my stomach contents.

I went back to my bed and curled up into a ball.

I was rushed to the hospital.

My wife of thirty years made the call.

I spent many hours in the emergency room.

I spent many days in a hospital room.

A few days in the recovery hospital,

Found me being moved to a new room.

They had moved me because my organs had shut down.

They thought I would die soon.

When things look the darkest,

When others think you have no hope,

A miraculous thing happens,

God intervenes.

Suddenly without warning everything reversed,

The organs started functioning.

The day dawned brighter for a wretched man.

God gave me second chance.

After many months of recovery I was again on my feet.

Paths soon made me cross God's plan for me.

I had been lost to the future that I had laid.

God's future saved me from my own plans and the grave.

My future is brighter

For now I see God's use of this piece of dust.

I shall not glory in my own accomplishments,

I shall give God the glory for saving me from me.

~~~~~~~~~~~~~~~~~~~

Spiritual Thoughts

Psalms 100

1 Make a joyful noise unto the LORD, all ye lands.

2 Serve the LORD with gladness: come before his presence with singing.

3 Know ye that the LORD he *is* God: *it is* he *that* hath made us, and not we ourselves; *we are* his people, and the sheep of his pasture.

4 Enter into his gates with thanksgiving, *and* into his courts with praise: be thankful unto him, *and* bless his name.

5 For the LORD *is* good; his mercy *is* everlasting; and his truth *endureth* to all generations.

~~~~~~~~~~~~~~~~~~~

Titles and Names of Christ

Advocate	Almighty	Arm of the Lord
Beloved Son	Bread of Life	Chef Sheppard
Corner Stone	Counselor	Deliverer
Door	Elect of God	Glory of the Lord
Good Sheppard	Great High Priest	Head of the Church
Holy One of God	Jesus	Just One
King of Kings	Lawgiver	Lamb of God
LifeLord of All	Man of Sorrows	
Mediator	Messiah	Morning Star
Only Begotten Son	Prince of Peace	Redeemer
Rock	Rose of Sharon	Savior
Son of Righteousness	True Light	Truth
Witness	Word	Word of God

Is there someone more important in your life than He?

~~~~~~~~~~~

Jesus at Your Door

If Jesus showed up at your door

And told you your work in this life is done

Would you be ready?

Would there be anything holding you back?

Life is temporary.

We must study, witness, and wait upon the Lord.

We must never be so busy we forget our duty to God.

We must be willing to lay down our lives and follow Him.

Life is short, and without purpose, if we follow after other things.

Material goods, self wants, and money are just temporary.

We came into this world naked.

We will leave with nothing but our soul.

Only the riches we build up in heaven will matter.

Jesus doesn't want us to be part time Christians.

He wants us on the job 24/7.

Jesus said you can't serve two masters.

Are you ready to serve The King of Kings?

~~~~~~~~~~~~~~~~~~~

Spiritual Thoughts

Heavenly Treasure

The Bible speaks of the treasure we have in heaven.

Whereas man thinks only of gold, gems, and material things.

God thinks of possessions you can not touch.

Peace, love, joy, kindness, eternal life.

I don't believe the riches in heaven are material.

I believe the riches in heaven are eternal.

Freedom of worry, sickness, evil, and other daily cares.

Eternally singing praises to God for His mercy.

It is a treasure we don't deserve.

It is a treasure paid for with His blood.

It is a treasure to be held for all eternity.

It is a treasure we are given freely.

~~~~~~~~~~~~~

The Valley of Despair

I sit in the valley of despair.

All around me mountains rise above.

They block out the sun.

And no man can help me.

Suddenly the mountains part.

The sun shines through.

I am saved from despair.

I am uplifted in a single moment.

The Word of God has spoken to me.

The way is clear for me to proceed.

I am no longer alone.

God has saved me.

When you are in a dark place,

And your spirits are low.

You can read the Book of Hope.

Just ask for wisdom to understand.

~~~~~~~~~~~~~~~~~~~

Nahum 1:7
The LORD *is* good, a stronghold in the day of trouble; and he knoweth them that trust in him.

Psalms 34:19
Many *are* the afflictions of the righteous: but the LORD delivereth him out of them all.

~~~~~~~~~~~~~~~~~~~

Spiritual Thoughts

The Church of Laodicea

Their church is large because the people are many.

Their good works are spread through out the community.

Their pastor preaches the gospel with much passion.

Their pastor then asks for forgiveness in case he offended.

They stay within the safety of their church.

They will not seek to win you with the gospel, only actions.

They have safety in their numbers.

They never spread their convictions lest you be hurt.

Come join them on Sunday and you will see their love.

Here their message of mercy.

See the love they have for each other.

You will not hear of "the fear of God".

If you are hurting they will take you in.

If you wish to join them you may

If you need to hear the truth you will.

Only keep it in your heart less it offends.

~~~~~~~~~~~~~~~~~~~~

Rev 3:14-22 (Jesus)

14 And unto the angel of the church of the Laodiceans write; These things saith the Amen, the faithful and true witness, the beginning of the creation of God;

15 I know thy works, that thou art neither cold nor hot: I would thou wert cold or hot.

16 So then because thou art lukewarm, and neither cold nor hot, I will spew thee out of my mouth.

17 Because thou sayest, I am rich, and increased with goods, and have need of nothing; and knowest not that thou art wretched, and miserable, and poor, and blind, and naked:

18 I counsel thee to buy of me gold tried in the fire, that thou mayest be rich; and white raiment, that thou mayest be clothed, and *that* the shame of thy nakedness do not appear; and anoint thine eyes with eye salve, that thou mayest see.

19 As many as I love, I rebuke and chasten: be zealous therefore, and repent.

20 Behold, I stand at the door, and knock: if any man hear my voice, and open the door, I will come in to him, and will sup with him, and he with me.

21 To him that overcometh will I grant to sit with me in my throne, even as I also overcame, and am set down with my Father in his throne.

22 He that hath an ear, let him hear what the Spirit saith unto the churches.

~~~~~~~~~~~~~~~~~

One Church

He brought them all together.

A one world church.

There were differences of structure and beliefs.

But they all agreed to live with tolerance for all.

(Continued Next Page)

Spiritual Thoughts

There were a few hold outs.

They believed in the love of God.

But they also believed in only One Way.

These few were the heretics of their day.

Now people could live without fear.

Now people could worship the way they wanted.

Now all could see a brighter tomorrow.

Only God disagreed.

~~~~~~~~~~~~~~~~~~~

John 14:6

Jesus saith unto him, I am the way, the truth, and the life: no man cometh unto the Father, but by me.

~~~~~~~~~~~~~~~

Pity Her

She has many tales of woe.

Her relatives are without honor.

No one does what she asks.

The whole world is against her.

She deals with untruths to justify her weakness.

She steals from others to ease her poor worth.

She clings to her faith although it is without righteousness.

She is alone from alienation.

Keep her daily in your prayers.

Pray she should find Jesus.

Pray for God to help her situation.

Pray for a soul lost

~~~~~~~~~~~~~~~~~~~

Proverbs 19:9

A false witness shall not be unpunished, and *he that* speaketh lies shall perish.

~~~~~~~~~~~~

Prayer - Matthew 6:9

Calling on God,

Creator, The Most Powerful, Our Father

Praise of Him

His greatness

Thanking Him

Petitions

(Continued Next Page)

Spiritual Thoughts

Intercession

Pleading

Counsel

Thanking Him

Seeking His will

Praise for His Kingdom

In Jesus' Name

~~~~~~~~~~~~~~~~~~~~~~~

Persecution

Should I worry because you think me mad?

Should I shrink into myself because you think I'm wrong?

Should I abandon my beliefs and follow the crowd?

Should your harsh words change my mind?

I have found Jesus.

He speaks to me daily and guides my steps.

I have safety, love, protection, inspiration.

I should never give these up for worldly pursuits.

Jesus suffered for His doctrine.

I shall not be sorry if I suffer for His sake.

I am protected from eternal damnation.

My reward can not be stolen.

My feet are set on high ground.

I shall not drown in a sea of sinfulness.

I can see my future, it is glorious.

My soul is protected, because I believe.

~~~~~~~~~~~~~~~~~~~

Rom 8:35 + 37

35 Who shall separate us from the love of Christ? *shall* tribulation, or distress, or persecution, or famine, or nakedness, or peril, or sword?
37 Nay, in all these things we are more than conquerors through him that loved us.

~~~~~~~~~~~~~~~~~~~

Look to Jesus

I watched the movie and took my eye off God.

I read the novel and took my eye off God.

I lusted after other women and took my eye off God.

I turned to sin because I took my eye off God.

Our enemy is deceitful.

He waits for us to fail.

We accommodate him when we divert our eyes away from God.

We fall when we loose sight of Jesus.

(Continued Next Page)

Spiritual Thoughts

Stay focused to the task.

Seek to study daily for His sake.

Be careful of becoming worldly.

Be happy, but be vigilant.

~~~~~~~~~~~~~~~~~~~

Psalms 1

1 Blessed *is* the man that walketh not in the counsel of the ungodly, nor standeth in the way of sinners, nor sitteth in the seat of the scornful.

2 But his delight *is* in the law of the LORD; and in his law doth he meditate day and night.

3 And he shall be like a tree planted by the rivers of water, that bringeth forth his fruit in his season; his leaf also shall not wither; and whatsoever he doeth shall prosper.

4 The ungodly *are* not so: but *are* like the chaff which the wind driveth away.

5 Therefore the ungodly shall not stand in the judgment, nor sinners in the congregation of the righteous.

6 For the LORD knoweth the way of the righteous: but the way of the ungodly shall perish.

~~~~~~~~~~~~~~~~

My Constant Friend

The first thing in the morning,

The last thing at night,

A daily walk by His side.

Mentioning Him in conversation.

Reciting a verse to cover the situation.

Praying for a friend or stranger whenever the need arises.

Working daily to increase the kingdom.

Keep Jesus & God with you daily.

Never forgetting the sacrifice or your unworthiness.

~~~~~~~~~~~~~~~~~~~

Seeking Others for Jesus

I share the truth,

Yet they hear me not.

I find ears turned to other doctrines.

I am not alone in sharing my faith.

Others have found what they were searching for.

Should I abandon them to their fate?

Should I try to turn them to the truth?

They feel they are right and will not turn.

I am sorrowful for them,

But God has told me of the broad way that leads to destruction.

And I know as many as will not turn are lost.

I can only pray for them.

(Continued Next Page)

Spiritual Thoughts

My heart aches for loved ones who will not listen.

I ask God daily for their hearts to turn to Him.

I seek wisdom to try to steer them into His path.

I know I must stay the course.

The end is coming.

I can see events bringing this life to a close.

I am constantly trying to rescue those I can.

I only pray that time doesn't run out.

Make your choice now for Jesus.

Don't wait for the end.

Only God knows the exact time.

Better Joy with Jesus than Death with the Devil.

~~~~~~~~~~~~~~~~~~

1Corinthians 15:51-54&57

51 Behold, I show you a mystery; We shall not all sleep, but we shall all be changed,

52 In a moment, in the twinkling of an eye, at the last trump: for the trumpet shall sound, and the dead shall be raised incorruptible and we shall be changed.

53 For this corruptible must put on incorruption, and this mortal *must* put on immortality.

54 So when this corruptible shall have put on incorruption, and this mortal shall have put on immortality, then shall be brought to pass the saying that is written, Death is swallowed up in victory.

57 But thanks *be* to God, which giveth us the victory through our Lord Jesus Christ.

~~~~~~~~~~~~~~~~~~~

Marriage

Did you listen carefully to your vows?

Did you marry for love only?

Do you remember for richer or poorer, in sickness, in health?

Will you keep the vows you said before God?

Help each other to keep your relationship with God.

Seek God's direction in both your lives.

Follow scripture to stay together.

The family that prays together, stays together.

Men, do you pray daily for your wife?

Do you "date" or otherwise surprise her?

Do you listen to her day?

Is she truly one with you?

~~~~~~~~~~~~~~~~~~~

(Continued Next Page)

Spiritual Thoughts

Eph 5:22-33

22 Wives, submit yourselves unto your own husbands, as unto the Lord.

23 For the husband is the head of the wife, even as Christ is the head of the church: and he is the savior of the body.

24 Therefore as the church is subject unto Christ, so *let* the wives *be* to their own husbands in every thing.

25 Husbands, love your wives, even as Christ also loved the church, and gave himself for it;

26 That he might sanctify and cleanse it with the washing of water by the word,

27 That he might present it to himself a glorious church, not having spot, or wrinkle, or any such thing; but that it should be holy and without blemish.

28 So ought men to love their wives as their own bodies. He that loveth his wife loveth himself.

29 For no man ever yet hated his own flesh; but nourisheth and cherisheth it, even as the Lord the church:

30 For we are members of his body, of his flesh, and of his bones.

31 For this cause shall a man leave his father and mother, and shall be joined unto his wife, and they two shall be one flesh.

32 This is a great mystery: but I speak concerning Christ and the church.

33 Nevertheless let every one of you in particular so love his wife even as himself; and the wife *see* that she reverence *her* husband.

~~~~~~~~~~~~~~~~~~~~~~~~~

From Christine S.

If your Bible is falling apart - your life isn't

~~~~~~~~~~~~~~~~~~~

Blinded By Satan

I speak, but he does not hear.

I preach the gospel, but he does not understand.

I show God's glory, but my words fall on deaf ears.

There is a glaze put over his eyes

We need to pray for the veil to be lifted.

We know God wants all to find salvation.

We know the Kingdom will be increased.

We are hindered by dark spiritual forces.

God will lift the veil.

We must have confidence.

We must have faith.

We must trust in Him.

~~~~~~~~~~~~~~~~~~

2Corinthians 3:16-17

16 Nevertheless when it shall turn to the Lord, the veil shall be taken away.

17 Now the Lord is that Spirit: and where the Spirit of the Lord *is,* there *is* liberty.

~~~~~~~~~~~~~~~~~~

Spiritual Thoughts

Trust God

My enemies encompass me.

They are armed with fear and worry.

They feed on my emotions and attack my mind.

Should I surrender to their attacks?

No! For my God is greater.

I shall not fear today or tomorrow.

I call on His strength and wisdom.

I fear nothing, for He is my refuge.

When problems come, do not trust self.

You may think you can solve them,

But trust God to solve them for you.

His power is greater and His love for you immense.

~~~~~~~~~~~~~~~~~~~

Romans 8: 31 what shall we then say to these things? If God *be* for us, who *can be* against us?

~~~~~~~~~~~~~~~~~~~~~~~

Trust

Should I trust the doctrine of men?

The person who says to trust in Mohammad.

The person who says to trust in Buddha.

The person who says to trust a man who intercepts plates.

The person who prays God, angels, and the saints.

The person who changes scripture to bolster his beliefs.

I must trust the Word of God and its promises.

The Word of God based on the ancient manuscripts.

The Word of God that speaks of Jesus Christ.

The Word of God that tells of His sacrifice for me.

The Word of God that tells us of the One Way.

The Word of God that tells the truth about salvation.

Seek the truth.

Trust in God.

Ask for His direction.

Accept Christ.

Live for Him.

Rejoice in Him.

~~~~~~~~~~~~~~~~~~~

Spiritual Thoughts

Proverbs 3:5-6

5 Trust in the LORD with all thine heart; and lean not unto thine own understanding.

6 In all thy ways acknowledge him, and he shall direct thy paths.

~~~~~~~~~~~~~~~~~~~~~~~~

Truth

Psalm 34:13-22

13 Keep thy tongue from evil, and thy lips from speaking guile.

14 Depart from evil, and do good; seek peace, and pursue it.

15 The eyes of the LORD *are* upon the righteous, and his ears *are open* unto their cry.

16 The face of the LORD *is* against them that do evil, to cut off the remembrance of them from the earth.

17 *The righteous* cry, and the LORD heareth, and delivereth them out of all their troubles.

18 The LORD *is* nigh unto them that are of a broken heart; and saveth such as be of a contrite spirit.

19 Many *are* the afflictions of the righteous: but the LORD delivereth him out of them all.

20 He keepeth all his bones: not one of them is broken.

21 Evil shall slay the wicked: and they that hate the righteous shall be desolate.

22 The LORD redeemeth the soul of his servants: and none of them that trust in him shall be desolate.

~~~~~~~~~~~~~~~~~~~~

Two Masters

I want to do good.

I seek those things which shall make me acceptable to God.

I work in a soup kitchen to help the poor.

I give to those in need.

I try to hold on to my former life.

My friends will not understand my change.

Therefore, I hide my new life.

I am not comfortable with my situation.

I wrestle with the situation of unanswered prayer.

I get on my knees each night,

But God doesn't seem to be listening.

I cry out to my church friends for answers.

~~~~~~~~~~~~~~~~~~~

Luke 16:13 No servant can serve two masters: for either he will hate the one, and love the other; or else he will hold to the one, and despise the other. Ye cannot serve God and mammon. (Jesus)

~~~~~~~~~~~~~~~

Choices

We enter this world with nothing.

We leave this world with only our souls.

In between, we make choices.

(Continued Next Page)

Spiritual Thoughts

Good or evil, right or wrong.

Living for God, living for self.

Accepting Jesus, or rejecting Him.

Please make the right choice.

Accepting Jesus, and living for God

Are the only things worthwhile?

Earthly gains become another's.

Evil choices become eternal damnation.

A moment of fleshly pleasure can become eternity without God.

~~~~~~~~~~~~~~~~~~~~

Titus 2:12-15

12 Teaching us that, denying ungodliness and worldly lusts, we should live soberly, righteously, and godly, in this present world;

13 Looking for that blessed hope, and the glorious appearing of the great God and our Savior Jesus Christ;

14 Who gave himself for us, that he might redeem us from all iniquity, and purify unto himself a peculiar people, zealous of good works.

15 These things speak, and exhort, and rebuke with all authority. Let no man despise thee.

~~~~~~~~~~~~~~~~~~~~

Because He Is

Standing alone with enemies all around,

Do not despair God is with you.

When others cause you pain,

Forgive them, for God does.

When faced with danger,

Stand tall God is your strength.

There is no suffering that God does not see.

There is no situation that God cannot fix.

There is no problem too big for the Creator of all.

There is strength in His Word.

There is comfort in His knowledge.

There is justice in His ending.

We cannot always understand His ways.

But we can be assured He will always be there for us.

We cannot always see tomorrow,

But we can be assured He will take care of its problems.

We do not always have the strength to carry on,

But He provides us with His strength.

~~~~~~~~~~~~~~~~~~~~

Micah 7:8-9

8 Rejoice not against me, O mine enemy: when I fall, I shall arise; when I sit in darkness, the LORD *shall be* a light unto me.

(Continued Next Page)

Spiritual Thoughts

9 I will bear the indignation of the LORD, because I have sinned against him, until he plead my cause, and execute judgment for me: he will bring me forth to the light, *and* I shall behold his righteousness.

Psalm 84:11-12

11 For the LORD God *is* a sun and shield: the LORD will give grace and glory: no good *thing* will he withhold from them that walk uprightly.

12 O LORD of hosts, blessed *is* the man that trusteth in thee.

2Corinthians 1:3-5

3 Blessed *be* God, even the Father of our Lord Jesus Christ, the Father of mercies, and the God of all comfort;

4 Who comforteth us in all our tribulation, that we may be able to comfort them which are in any trouble, by the comfort wherewith we ourselves are comforted of God.

5 For as the sufferings of Christ abound in us, so our consolation also aboundeth by Christ.

~~~~~~~~~~~~~~~~~~~~~~~

A Life Well Lived

He worked hard to provide for his family.

He lusted for no other but his wife.

He taught his children the ways of God.

He prayed with his family daily.

He attended church regularly.

His tithes and offerings were generous.

He gave much time to helping others.

He was outstanding in his community.

He was not ashamed of his belief in God.

He was vocal of his beliefs to everyone.

He gave out tracts at every opportunity.

His stand on God was evident.

He passed away suddenly.

He was mourned by many.

He left a legacy of love and devotion.

He went to heaven by Grace.

~~~~~~~~~~~~~~~~~~~~

Eph 2:8-9

8 For by grace are ye saved through faith; and that not of yourselves: *it is* the gift of God:

9 Not of works, lest any man should boast.

~~~~~~~~~~~~~~~~

Man's Theories VS God's Facts

His only facts are theories.

His only truths are imagination.

His knowledge is based on man's assessment.

His only destiny is the grave.

(Continued Next Page)

Spiritual Thoughts

When we look to ourselves,

We find ego, pride, and self.

When we look to ourselves,

We find weakness, and sin.

When we depart from scripture,

We can only surmise.

When we depart from God,

We lose salvation and hope.

~~~~~~~~~~~~~~~~~~~~

Luke 16:15

And he said unto them, Ye are they which justify yourselves before men; but God knoweth your hearts: for that which is highly esteemed among men is abomination in the sight of God. (Jesus)

~~~~~~~~~~~~~~~~~~~~

The Armor of God

Truth:

> Reading God's word daily.
>
> Trusting it for accuracy and never doubting its words.
>
> Seeking ways to use it in His service.
>
> Holding it in my heart for strength.

Righteousness:

    Seeking to be Christ-like.

    Standing for that which is right.

    Never seeking the ways of the world.

    Constantly vigilant to rid my heart of sin.

Gospel of peace.

    Knowing that God will provide me with His gifts.

    Knowing that I am just a pilgrim here.

    Trusting God will lead me to others for His sake.

    Setting my desire on heavenly things.

Faith:

    Believing in a Christ who died for me.

    Believing scripture as the actual Word of God.

    Believing in things not seen, words only uttered in my mind.

    Believing in a judgmental God.

Salvation:

    Accepting Jesus as the Son of the Living God.

    Knowing He shed His blood that I may have life.

    Calling Him Master and King.

    Picking up my cross to follow Him.

(Continued Next Page)

Spiritual Thoughts

Word of God:

> Believing that it is the unchanged word of the Master.

> Studying it, seeking its truths.

> Using it to lead others to Him.

> Resting on its promises of eternal life.

Prayer:

> Talking with the most powerful being in the entire universe.

> Praising Him, thanking Him, seeking His help,

> Ending with the name of our intercessor.

> Conversation with Our Heavenly Father, friend, constant help.

Eph. 6:13-18

13 Wherefore take unto you the whole armor of God, that ye may be able to withstand in the evil day, and having done all, to stand.

14 Stand therefore, having your loins girt about with truth, and having on the breastplate of righteousness;

15 And your feet shod with the preparation of the gospel of peace;

16 Above all, taking the shield of faith, wherewith ye shall be able to quench all the fiery darts of the wicked.

17 And take the helmet of salvation, and the sword of the Spirit, which is the word of God:

18 Praying always with all prayer and supplication in the Spirit, and watching thereunto with all perseverance and supplication for all saints;

~~~~~~~~~~~~~~~~~~~~~

Then and Now

Long before you taught us,

We brought pagan gods into our house.

We played with Ouija boards.

We studied yoga.

We fed our earthly desires.

We spoke against our neighbors.

Now we find pleasure in only heavenly pursuits.

Your scripture teaches us to put away idols.

Satan's diversions are no longer a temptation.

Other religions hold no interest.

Things of this world have been removed from our hearts.

Love has replaced gossip and speculation.

Teach us, O Lord, to find your truths.

May we respect you as our father.

Let us turn our hearts to your truths.

Let us continue to study your Word for strength.

May we keep our hearts turned always toward you.

Let love of all people be our hearts desire.

~~~~~~~~~~~~~~~~~~~~

Spiritual Thoughts

Romans 12:9-10

9 *Let* love be without dissimulation. Abhor that which is evil; cleave to that which is good.

10 *Be* kindly affectionate one to another with brotherly love; in honor preferring one another;

~~~~~~~~~~~~~~~~~~~

Riches

When you are wealthy in Jesus

Your wealth is not silver and gold.

It is measured in love, peace, contentment.

It is knowing He is watching over you.

Wealth can not give you love,

Like a mate who serves you even as you serve them,

Or friends that care for you as much as themselves,

Or His love that cares for an injured you.

Wealth can not give you peace,

Like knowing all your cares disappear when trusting Him,

Or seeing the beauty of the world He created,

Or in the knowledge of your next life in His presence.

Wealth can not give you contentment,

Like knowing each problem He will solve,

Or fully trusting in His grace,

Or toiling for Him to enlarge His kingdom.

~~~~~~~~~~~~~~~~~~~

LOVE

1Peter 1:22

Seeing ye have purified your souls in obeying the truth through the Spirit unto unfeigned love of the brethren, *see that ye* love one another with a pure heart fervently:

PEACE

Philippians 4:7

And the peace of God, which passeth all understanding, shall keep your hearts and minds through Christ Jesus.

CONTENTMENT

Philippians 4:11

Not that I speak in respect of want: for I have learned, in whatsoever state I am, *therewith* to be content.

~~~~~~~~~~~~~~~~~~~

(Continued Next Page)

Spiritual Thoughts

Progressive Miracles

You find a lost soul.

God lifts the veil of a lost soul.

A lost soul finds Christ.

You accept Jesus.

You work for His Kingdom.

You spend eternity with the King of Kings.

God gives you extra money.

God shows you a need for this money

God anticipates a future need.

You pray to God.

You listen for God.

God speaks to you.

You read scripture.

God reveals its secrets.

Your walk with God becomes closer.

~~~~~~~~~~~~~~~~~~~

Isaiah 65:24

And it shall come to pass, that before they call, I will answer; and while they are yet speaking, I will hear.

~~~~~~~~~~~~~~~~~~~~

Psalms of Praise

Psalm 100

1. Make a joyful noise unto the LORD, all ye lands.

2 Serve the LORD with gladness: come before his presence with singing.

3 Know ye that the LORD he *is* God: *it is* he *that* hath made us, and not we ourselves; *we are* his people, and the sheep of his pasture.

4 Enter into his gates with thanksgiving, *and* into his courts with praise: be thankful unto him, *and* bless his name.

5 For the LORD *is* good; his mercy *is* everlasting; and his truth *endureth* to all generations.

Psalm 117

1 O praise the LORD, all ye nations: praise him, all ye people.

2 For his merciful kindness is great toward us: and the truth of the LORD *endureth* forever. Praise ye the LORD.

~~~~~~~~~~~~~~~~~~~

Judgment Day

I hung my head as the verdict was read.

I had committed all of these things knowingly.

I could not deny any of the charges against me.

I waited for my judgment.

(Continued Next Page)

Spiritual Thoughts

When the verdict came I was joyful in my heart.

I had committed all these wrongs, yet I was free!

I was free because of Him.

I was free because long ago I accepted Him.

I was born with a sinful nature.

I finally admitted my guilt and asked for forgiveness.

As I lived after His forgiveness, I still had a sinful nature.

I fought my nature and through His strength over came.

I live daily knowing God's strength and mercy.

I continue to look deep in my heart for darkness.

His light will overcome all darkness.

All you have to do is ask.

You too can escape an eternity without Jesus.

Realize He bled and died for you.

Accept Him and ask for His forgiveness.

His mercy will keep you from joining Satan in the pit.

~~~~~~~~~~~~~~~~~~~~

Matt. 12:36-37 (Jesus)

36 But I say unto you, That every idle word that men shall speak, they shall give account thereof in the day of judgment.

37 For by thy words thou shalt be justified, and by thy words thou shalt be condemned.

Rom. 14:8-10

8 For whether we live, we live unto the Lord; and whether we die, we die unto the Lord: whether we live therefore, or die, we are the Lord's.

9 For to this end Christ both died, and rose, and revived, that he might be Lord both of the dead and living.

10 But why dost thou judge thy brother or why dost thou set at naught thy brother? For we shall all stand before the judgment seat of Christ.

2Cor. 5:10

For we must all appear before the judgment seat of Christ; that every one may receive the things *done* in *his* body, according to that he hath done, whether *it be* good or bad.

~~~~~~~~~~~~~~~~~~~

The New Covenant

From the dust of the earth God formed man.

God walked with man.

God gave man a choice.

God loved His creation.

After the fall, mankind started going his own way.

Man became full of vanity and drew away from God.

He labored for himself and forgot his creator.

God reached into his heart and found wickedness.

(Continued Next Page)

Spiritual Thoughts

God decided to destroy His creation.

Except for Noah and His family, all were drowned.

The earth started over with thankfulness.

All was new and life looked bright.

As mankind continued on his journey,

Again God reached into man's heart and found wickedness.

A few stayed true to the creator,

But the many stayed with their iniquity.

God sent His last Hope for mankind.

God sent His Son that through Him

We would find salvation.

His blood, shed for us, cleansed us from our sin.

God broke the bonds of His first covenant with Abraham.

His new covenant provided One Way to eternity.

Mankind could now choose the narrow or the broad path.

Mankind had The Example to follow.

Jesus paid the price for our sin.

God's perfect plan can not be sidestepped.

There is only One Way.

There is only one Jesus.

~~~~~~~~~~~~~~~~~~~~

Zechariah 11:9-10

9 Then said I, I will not feed you: that that dieth, let it die; and that that is to be cut off, let it be cut off; and let the rest eat every one the flesh of another.

10 And I took my staff, *even* Beauty, and cut it asunder, that I might break my covenant which I had made with all the people.

~~~~~~~~~~~~~~~~~~~~

Redeemed

I walked a road of darkness.

I cared for only myself.

My hopes were for the future I would build.

My thoughts were not pure.

I went to church to please another.

I was sure I could resist its call.

My heart was not seeking salvation.

My thoughts were on self and wickedness.

(Continued Next Page)

Spiritual Thoughts

The speaker was loud and forceful.

The words were speaking to my heart.

The songs spoke to my soul.

The invitation carried me to the front.

I only went to church to please another.

I didn't go to please God.

Jesus found me in His house.

Jesus accepted me as I was.

I now thank God for rescuing me from me.

I now thank Him for His Son.

I now thank Him for my new life.

I now thank Him for His servants who cared for me.

Reach out and touch the Savior.

Reach out and touch Our Friend.

Reach out and touch another.

Reach out and help the lost.

~~~~~~~~~

Psalm 126:5-6

5 They that sow in tears shall reap in joy.

6 He that goeth forth and weepeth, bearing precious seed, shall doubtless come again with rejoicing, bringing his sheaves *with him*.

~~~~~~~~~~~~~~~~~~~

Lost or Saved

Proverbs 1:22-33

22 How long, ye simple ones, will ye love simplicity? And the scorners delight in their scorning, and fools hate knowledge?

23 Turn you at my reproof: behold, I will pour out my spirit unto you, I will make known my words unto you.

24 Because I have called, and ye refused; I have stretched out my hand, and no man regarded;

25 But ye have set at naught all my counsel, and would none of my reproof:

26 I also will laugh at your calamity; I will mock when your fear cometh;

27 When your fear cometh as desolation, and your destruction cometh as a whirlwind; when distress and anguish cometh upon you.

28 Then shall they call upon me, but I will not answer; they shall seek me early, but they shall not find me:

29 For that they hated knowledge, and did not choose the fear of the LORD:

30 They would none of my counsel: they despised all my reproof.

31 Therefore shall they eat of the fruit of their own way, and be filled with their own devices.

32 For the turning away of the simple shall slay them, and the prosperity of fools shall destroy them.

33 But whoso hearkeneth unto me shall dwell safely, and shall be quiet from fear of evil.

Proverbs 2:1-11

1 My son, if thou wilt receive my words, and hide my commandments with thee;

(Continued Next Page)

Spiritual Thoughts

2 So that thou incline thine ear unto wisdom, *and* apply thine heart to understanding;

3 Yea, if thou criest after knowledge, *and* liftest up thy voice for understanding;

4 If thou seekest her as silver, and searchest for her as *for* hid treasures;

5 Then shalt thou understand the fear of the LORD, and find the knowledge of God.

6 For the LORD giveth wisdom: out of his mouth *cometh* knowledge and understanding.

7 He layeth up sound wisdom for the righteous: *he is* a buckler to them that walk uprightly.

8 He keepeth the paths of judgment, and preserveth the way of his saints.

9 Then shalt thou understand righteousness, and judgment, and equity; *yea*, every good path.

10 When wisdom entereth into thine heart, and knowledge is pleasant unto thy soul;

11 Discretion shall preserve thee, understanding shall keep thee:

~~~~~~~~~~~~~~~~~~~

Just a Man

My thoughts are not pure.

My mouth speaks vile things.

My eyes do not divert from lust.

My actions sometimes not Christ-like.

I am a man with a sinful past.

I am a man who stumbles at times.

I am not perfect.

I am continuing to grow in grace.

I read His word daily.

I mediate on His scripture.

I pray for constant help.

I need to shed my past and seek a new tomorrow.

God is gracious and merciful.

He can help me from myself.

The Holy Spirit continues to clean my heart.

I continue to seek God's forgiveness.

I can admit to my weakness,

For God is my strength.

I can submit to His mercy,

For God is love.

~~~~~~~~~~~~~~~~~~~

John 14:16-17 (Jesus)

16 And I will pray the Father, and he shall give you another Comforter, that he may abide with you forever;

17 *Even* the Spirit of truth; whom the world cannot receive, because it seeth him not, neither knoweth him: but ye know him; for he dwelleth with you, and shall be in you.

(Continued Next Page)

Spiritual Thoughts

Romans 6:1-2

1 What shall we say then? Shall we continue in sin, that grace may abound?

2 God forbid. How shall we, that are dead to sin, live any longer therein?

Romans 6:14-15

14 For sin shall not have dominion over you: for ye are not under the law, but under grace.

15 What then? Shall we sin, because we are not under the law, but under grace? God forbid

Proverbs 3:6 In all thy ways acknowledge him, and he shall direct thy paths.

2Timothy 2:15 Study to show thyself approved unto God, a workman that needeth not to be ashamed, rightly dividing the word of truth.

~~~~~~~~~~~~~~~~~~~~

Who is like unto our God?

He is the Father of Lights.

His radiance shines down upon us

Like the sun of a spring day.

It baths us in its warmth.

Man creates mischief.

God creates all living things.

He touches the mountains and they smoke.

He can make a storm or calm.

Problems arise within our lives,

But He is there to solve our problems.

He can provide for us even before we ask.

He can heal and strengthen us.

God has given us life and spirit.

Man can create life but not spirit.

God can send our spirit soaring during our triumphs.

God can call this spirit back to him at our end.

Man can build much wealth,

But God can take it away.

Man can be poor in wealth,

But God can give him riches not seen.

Who is like unto our God?

Would you be willing to give your child

Into the hands of the enemy

To be beaten and nailed to a cross?

(Continued Next Page)

Spiritual Thoughts

Is there no greater love than this?

Is there no greater sacrifice?

God is merciful.

God is grace.

God is fear and terror to the unsaved.

God is mighty in deed.

God is powerful in His doings.

God is just in His judgments.

From God we receive strength when we are weak.

From God we receive love to share with others.

From God we find peace in time of trouble.

From God we find hope for the future.

God will prevail.

God's predictions will come true.

God will have the final say.

God is Alpha and Omega.

Only God knows our hearts.

Only God can create without defect.

Only God can show forth might and yet save the sparrow.

Only God governs our destiny.

Through Adam He gave us creation.

Through Noah He gave us a fresh start.

Through Abraham He gave us a place in the world.

Through Jesus He gave us eternal life.

There is none like unto our God.

We can not save ourselves.

Our Spirit belongs to the Creator.

Our lives belong to the Master of the Universe.

Man's gods will fail.

Man's ambitions come to naught without Him.

Man is nothing without His Power.

Man can not compare with His infinite wisdom.

~~~~~~~~~~~~~~~~~~~

Matthew 19:26 But Jesus beheld *them,* and said unto them, with men this is impossible; but with God all things are possible.

Luke 3:8 Bring forth therefore fruits worthy of repentance, and begin not to say within yourselves, We have Abraham to *our* father: for I say unto you, That God is able of these stones to raise up children unto Abraham.

Psalm 95:3 For the LORD *is* a great God, and a great King above all gods.

Psalm 27:1 The LORD *is* my light and my salvation; whom shall I fear? The LORD *is* the strength of my life; of whom shall I be afraid?

~~~~~~~~~~~~~~~~~~~

Spiritual Thoughts

Hollywood Hype verses Scripture Sense

Hollywood Hype

After death there is either reincarnation or a body that responds without a soul.

Scripture Sense

Genesis 3:19 In the sweat of thy face shalt thou eat bread, till thou return unto the ground; for out of it wast thou taken: for dust thou *art*, and unto dust shalt thou return.

Hollywood Hype

Deceit, sex without marriage, even murder is acceptable if you are the hero.

Scripture Sense

Galatians 5:19-21

19 Now the works of the flesh are manifest, which are *these*; adultery, fornication, uncleanness, lasciviousness,

20 Idolatry, witchcraft, hatred, variance, emulations, wrath, strife, seditions, heresies,

21 Envying, murders, drunkenness, reveling, and such like: of which I tell you before, as I have also told *you* in time past, that they which do such things shall not inherit the kingdom of God.

Hollywood Hype

If you are good you will go to heaven.

Scripture Sense

Romans 5:17-18

17 For if by one man's offense death reigned by one; much more they which receive abundance of grace and of the gift of righteousness shall reign in life by one, Jesus Christ.

18 Therefore as by the offense of one *judgment came* upon all men to condemnation; even so by the righteousness of one *the free gift came* upon all men unto justification of life.

Romans 10:13 For whosoever shall call upon the name of the Lord shall be saved.

~~~~~~~~~~~~~~~~~~~~

The Enemy Within

A couple wishes to join the efforts of another church.

God has opened an opportunity for them to share in His work.

Their own pastor tells them,

"We can't support you since it isn't tied to our church."

God's agenda has been replaced by pride.

The enemy has come within their midst.

A couple brings their newborn to the front of the assembly.

They wish to publicly give her up to the Lord.

Their pastor tells them,

"We will have to do this in another service."

Pageantry has taken over spontaneity.

The enemy has come within their midst.

(Continued Next Page)

Spiritual Thoughts

The assembly has become divided.

The man of God uses scripture to reason both sides.

One side will not be moved.

The assembly is ripped apart with some standing with the pastor.

Reasoning has been replaced by Pride.

The enemy has come within their midst.

~~~~~~~~~~~~~~~~~~~~

1 John 3:7-8

7 Little children, let no man deceive you: he that doeth righteousness is righteous, even as he is righteous.

8 He that committeth sin is of the devil; for the devil sinneth from the beginning. For this purpose the Son of God was manifested, that he might destroy the works of the devil.

~~~~~~~~~~~~~~~~~~~~

1Peter 5:8-11

8 Be sober, be vigilant; because your adversary the devil, as a roaring lion, walketh about, seeking whom he may devour:

9 Whom resist steadfast in the faith, knowing that the same afflictions are accomplished in your brethren that are in the world.

10 But the God of all grace, who hath called us unto his eternal glory by Christ Jesus, after that ye have suffered a while, make you perfect, establish, strengthen, settle *you*.

11 To him *be* glory and dominion forever and ever. Amen.

~~~~~~~~~~~~~~~~~~~~

Study His Word

God feeds me daily, and I hunger for more.

His meat is the Word of God.

Other books He shows me to increase my knowledge.

Christian music helps to excite, calm, and refresh my soul.

The more time I spend with Christian teachings

The stronger I become for His service.

I need His acceptance and continually seek His will.

I need to serve Him more fully.

The knowledge He gives helps to expand His kingdom.

The brethren He lets me meet renews my drive.

The church is my constant strength.

His wisdom my constant help.

The most important part of my day

Is when I read and study His word.

I see verses with such clarity.

I long for this time and for His presence.

(Continued Next Page)

Spiritual Thoughts

His Word: brings light into the darkness

exposes the lies of our enemy.

refreshes, calms, and nourishes us.

is the first place I turn for answers.

~~~~~~~~~~~~~~~~~~

Psalm 119:97 -105

97 O how love I thy law! It *is* my meditation all the day.

98 Thou through thy commandments hast made me wiser than mine enemies: for they *are* ever with me.

99 I have more understanding than all my teachers: for thy testimonies *are* my meditation.

100 I understand more than the ancients, because I keep thy precepts.

101 I have refrained my feet from every evil way, that I might keep thy word.

102 I have not departed from thy judgments: for thou hast taught me.

103 How sweet are thy words unto my taste! *Yea, sweeter* than honey to my mouth!

104 Through thy precepts I get understanding therefore I hate every false way.

105 Thy word *is* a lamp unto my feet, and a light unto my path.

~~~~~~~~~~~~~~~~~~

Satan's Deceit

Our enemy has many names.

His ways are unlike our Lord.

He seeks to kill, steal, or destroy God's children.

He is jealous of the Creator.

He has built many ways to deceive.

His seen gods are made by the hand of man.

His hidden gods are made by the mind of man.

He has skillfully copied many of God's creations.

Though we sometimes think we have found salvation,

There is only One Way.

Though we puff ourselves up,

There is only one God.

How long will we deceive ourselves?

How many times will we follow false gods?

How often will we choose the easy path?

How often will we snub the true God?

Lies believed will not stand.

Sin unforgiven will lead to eternal damnation.

Enemy obedience will destroy us.

Satan's enticements can lead us astray.

(Continued Next Page)

Spiritual Thoughts

Search the scriptures for the truth.

Seek our God for the answers.

Search your heart for obedience to God's will.

Seek salvation in the blood of Christ.

~~~~~~~~~~~~~~~~~~~

Luke 22:31-32

31 And the Lord said, Simon, Simon, behold, Satan hath desired *to have* you, that he may sift *you* as wheat:

32 But I have prayed for thee, that thy faith fail not: and when thou art converted, strengthen thy brethren.

1John 3:8

He that committeth sin is of the devil; for the devil sinneth from the beginning. For this purpose the Son of God was manifested, that he might destroy the works of the devil.

Ephesians 4:26-27

26 Be ye angry, and sin not: let not the sun go down upon your wrath:

27 Neither give place to the devil.

~~~~~~~~~~~~~~~~~~~

This last section is on the most famous sermon ever recorded. Because God's word is powerful enough without explanation, I let it stand for itself. After Chapter 5:1-2 I have broken this into sections with supporting commentary indented. Please ask God for help in understanding and divine wisdom to understand its meaning for you.

Sermon on the Mount

Matthew 5

1 And seeing the multitudes, he went up into a mountain: and when he was set, his disciples came unto him:

2 And he opened his mouth, and taught them, saying,

Characteristics of a Complete Christian

3 Blessed *are* the poor in spirit: for theirs is the kingdom of heaven.

4 Blessed *are* they that mourn: for they shall be comforted.

5 Blessed *are* the meek: for they shall inherit the earth.

6 Blessed *are* they which do hunger and thirst after righteousness: for they shall be filled.

7 Blessed *are* the merciful: for they shall obtain mercy.

8 Blessed *are* the pure in heart: for they shall see God.

9 Blessed *are* the peacemakers: for they shall be called the children of God.

10 Blessed *are* they which are persecuted for righteousness' sake: for theirs is the kingdom of heaven.

(Continued Next Page)

Spiritual Thoughts

11 Blessed are ye, when *men* shall revile you, and persecute *you,* and shall say all manner of evil against you falsely, for my sake.

12 Rejoice, and be exceeding glad: for great *is* your reward in heaven: for so persecuted they the prophets which were before you.

> **Luke 6:40** The disciple is not above his master: but every one that is perfect shall be as his master. (Jesus)
>
> **Ephesians. 4:12-13** For the perfecting of the saints, for the work of the ministry, for the edifying of the body of Christ:
>
> 13 Till we all come in the unity of the faith, and of the knowledge of the Son of God, unto a perfect man, unto the measure of the stature of the fullness of Christ:
>
> **2Corinthians 13:11** Finally, brethren, farewell. Be perfect, be of good comfort, be of one mind, live in peace; and the God of love and peace shall be with you.
>
> **2Timothy 3:16 - 17** All Scripture *is* given by inspiration of God, and *is* profitable for doctrine, for reproof, for correction, for instruction in righteousness:
>
> 17 That the man of God may be perfect thoroughly furnished unto all good works.

<u>Christian Influence</u>

13 Ye are the salt of the earth: but if the salt have lost his savor, wherewith shall it be salted? It is thenceforth good for nothing, but to be cast out, and to be trodden under foot of men.

> **Mark 9:50** Salt *is* good: but if the salt have lost his saltness, wherewith will ye season it? Have salt in yourselves and have peace one with another. (Jesus)
>
>   ***salt***: figuratively *prudence: worth*

Be a Light

14 Ye are the light of the world. A city that is set on a hill cannot be hid.

15 Neither do men light a candle, and put it under a bushel, but on a candlestick; and it giveth light unto all that are in the house.

16 Let your light so shine before men, that they may see your good works, and glorify your Father which is in heaven.

Ephesians 5:8 For ye were sometimes darkness, but now *are ye* light in the Lord: walk as children of light:

Colossians 1:10 That ye might walk worthy of the Lord unto all pleasing, being fruitful in every good work, and increasing in the knowledge of God;

John 15:8 Herein is my Father glorified, that ye bear much fruit; so shall ye be my disciples. (Jesus)

Christ & the Law

17 Think not that I am come to destroy the law, or the prophets: I am not come to destroy, but to fulfill.

18 For verily I say unto you, Till heaven and earth pass, one jot or one title shall in no wise pass from the law, till all be fulfilled.

19 he shall be called the least in the kingdom of heaven: but whosoever shall do and teach *them,* the same shall be called great in the kingdom of heaven.

20 For I say unto you, That except your righteousness shall exceed *the righteousness* of the scribes and Pharisees, ye shall in no case enter into the kingdom of heaven.

Acts 7:37 -38 This is that Moses, which said unto the children of Israel, A prophet shall the Lord your God raise up unto you of your brethren, like unto me; him shall ye hear.

(Continued Next Page)

38 This is he, that was in the church in the wilderness with the angel which spake to him in the mount Sinai, and *with* our fathers: who received the lively oracles to give unto us:

Spiritual Principle

21 Ye have heard that it was said by them of old time, Thou shalt not kill; and whosoever shall kill shall be in danger of the judgment:

22 But I say unto you, That whosoever is angry with his brother without a cause shall be in danger of the judgment: and whosoever shall say to his brother, Raca, shall be in danger of the council: but whosoever shall say, Thou fool, shall be in danger of hell fire.

23 Therefore if thou bring thy gift to the altar, and there rememberest that thy brother hath aught against thee;

24 Leave there thy gift before the altar, and go thy way; first be reconciled to thy brother, and then come and offer thy gift.

25 Agree with thine adversary quickly, while thou art in the way with him; lest at any time the adversary deliver thee to the judge, and the judge deliver thee to the officer, and thou be cast into prison.

26 Verily I say unto thee, Thou shalt by no means come out thence, till thou hast paid the uttermost farthing.

Colossians 3:8 But now ye also put off all these; anger, wrath, malice, blasphemy, filthy communication out of your mouth.

Titus 3:1-2

1 Put them in mind to be subject to principalities and powers, to obey magistrates, to be ready to every good work,

2 To speak evil of no man, to be no brawlers, *but* gentle, showing all meekness unto all men.

Inward Purity Required

27 Ye have heard that it was said by them of old time, Thou shalt not commit adultery:

28 But I say unto you, That whosoever looketh on a woman to lust after her hath committed adultery with her already in his heart.

29 And if thy right eye offend thee, pluck it out, and cast *it* from thee: for it is profitable for thee that one of thy members should perish, and not *that* thy whole body should be cast into hell.

30 And if thy right hand offend thee, cut it off, and cast *it* from thee: for it is profitable for thee that one of thy members should perish, and not *that* thy whole body should be cast into hell.

> **Romans 7:3** So then if, while *her* husband liveth, she be married to another man, she shall be called an adulteress: but if her husband be dead, she is free from that law; so that she is no adulteress, though she be married to another man.
>
> **Romans 13:14** But put ye on the Lord Jesus Christ, and make not provision for the flesh, to *fulfill* the lusts *thereof.*
>
> **Romans 6:6** Knowing this, that our old man is crucified with *him,* that the body of sin might be destroyed, that henceforth we should not serve sin.
>
> **Colossians 2:11** In whom also ye are circumcised with the circumcision made without hands, in putting off the body of the sins of the flesh by the circumcision of Christ:
>
> **Colossians 3:5** Mortify therefore your members which are upon the earth; fornication, uncleanness, inordinate affection, evil concupiscence, and covetousness, which is idolatry:

Spiritual Thoughts

Marriage Sacred

31 It hath been said, Whosoever shall put away his wife, let him give her a writing of divorcement:

32 But I say unto you, That whosoever shall put away his wife, saving for the cause of fornication, causeth her to commit adultery: and whosoever shall marry her that is divorced committeth adultery.

Matthew 19:7-9 They say unto him (Jesus), Why did Moses then command to give a writing of divorcement, and to put her away

8 He saith unto them, Moses because of the hardness of your hearts suffered you to put away your wives: but from the beginning it was not so.

9 And I say unto you, Whosoever shall put away his wife, except *it be* for fornication, and shall marry another, committeth adultery: and whoso marrieth her which is put away doth commit adultery.

Ephesians 5:25 Husbands love your wives, even as Christ also loved the church, and gave himself for it;

1Peter 3:7 Likewise, ye husbands, dwell with *them* according to knowledge, giving honor unto the wife, as unto the weaker vessel, and as being heirs together of the grace of life; that your prayers be not hindered.

Oaths Profanity

33 Again, ye have heard that it hath been said by them of old time, Thou shalt not forswear thyself, but shalt perform unto the Lord thine oaths:

34 But I say unto you, Swear not at all; neither by heaven; for it is God's throne:

35 Nor by the earth; for it is his footstool: neither by Jerusalem; for it is the city of the great King.

36 Neither shalt thou swear by thy head, because thou canst not make one hair white or black.

37 But let your communication be, Yea, yea; Nay, nay: for whatsoever is more than these cometh of evil.

Numbers 30:2 If a man vow a vow unto the LORD, or swear an oath to bind his soul with a bond; he shall not break his word, he shall do according to all that proceedeth out of his mouth.

Ecclesiastes 5:4 When thou vowest a vow unto God, defer not to pay it; for *he hath* no pleasure in fools: pay that which thou hast vowed.

Colossians 4:6 Let your speech *be* always with grace, seasoned with salt, that ye may know how ye ought to answer every man.

New Resistance Required

38 Ye have heard that it hath been said, An eye for an eye, and a tooth for a tooth:

39 But I say unto you, That ye resist not evil: but whosoever shall smite thee on thy right cheek, turn to him the other also.

40 And if any man will sue thee at the law, and take away thy coat, let him have *thy* cloak also.

Romans 12:17 Recompense to no man evil for evil. Provide things honest in the sight of all men.

Proverbs 20:22 Say not thou, I will recompense evil; *but* wait on the LORD, and he shall save thee.

Ephesians 6:9 And, ye masters, do the same things unto them, forbearing threatening: knowing that your Master also is in heaven; neither is there respect of persons with him.

Colossians 3:13 Forbearing one another, and forgiving one another, if any man have a quarrel against any: even as Christ forgave you, so also *do* ye.

Unlimited Service

41 And whosoever shall compel thee to go a mile, go with him twain.

(Continued Next Page)

Spiritual Thoughts

42 Give to him that asketh thee, and from him that would borrow of thee turn not thou away.

2Corinthians 8:12 For[1] if there be first a willing mind, *it is* accepted according to that a man hath, *and* not according to that he hath not.

2Corinthians 9:7 Every man according as he purposeth in his heart, *so let him give*; not grudgingly, or of necessity: for God loveth a cheerful giver.

Psalm 37:25-26

25 I have been young, and *now* am old; yet have I not seen the righteous forsaken, nor his seed begging bread.

26 *He is* ever merciful, and lendeth; and his seed *is* blessed.

The Christian Life Required

43 Ye have heard that it hath been said, Thou shalt love thy neighbor, and hate thine enemy.

44 But I say unto you, Love your enemies, bless them that curse you, do good to them that hate you, and pray for them which despitefully use you, and persecute you;

45 That ye may be the children of your Father which is in heaven: for he maketh his sun to rise on the evil and on the good, and sendeth rain on the just and on the unjust.

46 For if ye love them which love you, what reward have ye? do not even the publicans the same?

47 And if ye salute your brethren only, what do ye more *than others*? do not even the publicans so?

John 15:12 This is my commandment, That ye love one another, as I have loved you. (Jesus)

Romans 12:9 *Let* love be without dissimulation. Abhor that which is evil; cleave to that which is good.

1Thessalonians 3:12 And the Lord make you to increase and abound in love one toward another, and toward all *men,* even as we *do* toward you:

1Peter 1:22 Seeing ye have purified your souls in obeying the truth through the Spirit unto unfeigned love of the brethren, *see that ye* love one another with a pure heart fervently:

Divine Standard of Life

48 Be ye therefore perfect, even as your Father which is in heaven is perfect.

2Timothy 3:16-17

16 All Scripture *is* given by inspiration of God, and *is* profitable for doctrine, for reproof, for correction, for instruction in righteousness:

17 That the man of God may be perfect, thoroughly furnished unto all good works.

Hebrews13:21 Make you perfect in every good work to do his will, working in you that which is well pleasing in his sight, through Jesus Christ; to whom *be* glory forever and ever. Amen.

~~~~~~~~~~~~~~~~~~~

Matthew 6
<u>Doing Good</u>

1 Take heed that ye do not your alms before men, to be seen of them: otherwise ye have no reward of your Father which is in heaven.

2 Therefore when thou doest *thine* alms, do not sound a trumpet before thee, as the hypocrites do in the synagogues and in the streets, that they may have glory of men. Verily I say unto you, They have their reward.

3 But when thou doest alms, let not thy left hand know what thy right hand doeth:

4 That thine alms may be in secret: and thy Father which seeth in secret himself shall reward thee openly.

(Continued Next Page)

Spiritual Thoughts

Deuteronomy 15:7 If there be among you a poor man of one of thy brethren within any of thy gates in thy land which the LORD thy God giveth thee, thou shalt not harden thine heart, nor shut thine hand from thy poor brother:

Revelation 21:27 And there shall in no wise enter into it any thing that defileth, neither *whatsoever* worketh abomination, or *maketh* a lie: but they which are written in the Lamb's book of life.

Proverbs 23:6-7

6 Eat thou not the bread of *him that hath* an evil eye, neither desire thou his dainty meats:

7 For as he thinketh in his heart, so *is* he: Eat and drink, saith he to thee; but his heart *is* not with thee

Proverbs 11:2 *When* pride cometh, then cometh shame: but with the lowly *is* wisdom.

John 12:26 If any man serve me, let him follow me; and where I am, there shall also my servant be: if any man serve me, him will *my* Father honor. (Jesus)

1Samuel 2:3 Talk no more so exceeding proudly; let *not* arrogance come out of your mouth: for the LORD *is* a God of knowledge, and by him actions are weighed.

How To Pray

5 And when thou prayest, thou shalt not be as the hypocrites *are*: for they love to pray standing in the synagogues and in the corners of the streets, that they may be seen of men. Verily I say unto you, They have their reward.

6 But thou, when thou prayest, enter into thy closet, and when thou hast shut thy door, pray to thy Father which is in secret; and thy Father which seeth in secret shall reward thee openly.

7 But when ye pray, use not vain repetitions, as the heathen *do*: for they think that they shall be heard for their much speaking.

8 Be not ye therefore like unto them: for your Father knoweth what things ye have need of, before ye ask him.

Luke 18:10-14 (Jesus)

10 Two men went up into the temple to pray; the one a Pharisee, and the other a publican.

11 The Pharisee stood and prayed thus with himself, God, I thank thee, that I am not as other men *are,* extortioners, unjust, adulterers, or even as this publican.

12 I fast twice in the week, I give tithes of all that I possess.

13 And the publican, standing afar off, would not lift up so much as *his* eyes unto heaven, but smote upon his breast, saying, God be merciful to me a sinner.

14 I tell you, this man went down to his house justified *rather* than the other: for every one that exalteth himself shall be abased; and he that humbleth himself shall be exalted.

Psalms 91:15 He shall call upon me, and I will answer him: I *will be* with him in trouble; I will deliver him, and honor him.

Ecclesiastes 5:2 Be not rash with thy mouth, and let not thine heart be hasty to utter *any* thing before God: for God *is* in heaven, and thou upon earth: therefore let thy words be few.

2Timothy 3:5 Having a form of godliness, but denying the power thereof: from such turn away.

Psalms 121:3 He will not suffer thy foot to be moved: he that keepeth thee will not slumber.

The Lord's Prayer

9 After this manner therefore pray ye: Our Father which art in heaven, Hallowed be thy name.

10 Thy kingdom come. Thy will be done in earth, as *it is* in heaven.

11 Give us this day our daily bread.

12 And forgive us our debts, as we forgive our debtors.

13 And lead us not into temptation, but deliver us from evil: For thine is the kingdom, and the power, and the glory, forever. Amen.

(Continued Next Page)

Spiritual Thoughts

14 For if ye forgive men their trespasses, your heavenly Father will also forgive you:

15 But if ye forgive not men their trespasses, neither will your Father forgive your trespasses.

Ephesians 3:14 For this cause I bow my knees unto the Father of our Lord Jesus Christ,

Romans 6:12-13

12 Let not sin therefore reign in your mortal body, that ye should obey it in the lusts thereof.

13 Neither yield ye your members *as* instruments of unrighteousness unto sin: but yield yourselves unto God, as those that are alive from the dead, and your members *as* instruments of righteousness unto God.

Psalms 40:8 I delight to do thy will, O my God: yea, thy law *is* within my heart.

Psalms 25:11 For thy name's sake, O LORD, pardon mine iniquity; for it *is* great.

Daniel 6:27 He delivereth and rescueth, and he worketh signs and wonders in heaven and in earth, who hath delivered Daniel from the power of the lions.

1Chronicles 29:12 Both riches and honor *come* of thee, and thou reignest over all; and in thine hand *is* power and might; and in thine hand *it is* to make great, and to give strength unto all.

Ephesians 4:32 And be ye kind one to another, tenderhearted, forgiving one another, even as God for Christ's sake hath forgiven you.

Isaiah 58:10 And *if* thou draw out thy soul to the hungry, and satisfy the afflicted soul; then shall thy light rise in obscurity, and thy darkness *be* as the noonday:

How To Fast

16 Moreover when ye fast, be not, as the hypocrites, of a sad countenance: for they disfigure their faces, that they may appear unto men to fast. Verily I say unto you, They have their reward.

17 But thou, when thou fastest, anoint thine head, and wash thy face;

18 That thou appear not unto men to fast, but unto thy Father which is in secret: and thy Father, which seeth in secret, shall reward thee openly.

> **Matthew 9:15** And Jesus said unto them, Can the children of the bridechamber mourn, as long as the bridegroom is with them? but the days will come, when the bridegroom shall be taken from them, and then shall they fast.
>
> **1Samuel 16:7** But the LORD said unto Samuel, Look not on his countenance, or on the height of his stature; because I have refused him: for *the LORD seeth* not as man seeth; for man looketh on the outward appearance, but the LORD looketh on the heart.
>
> **1Timothy 6:16** Who only hath immortality, dwelling in the light which no man can approach unto; whom no man hath seen, nor can see: to whom *be* honor and power everlasting. Amen.
>
> **Romans 8:27** And he that searcheth the hearts knoweth what *is* the mind of the Spirit, because he maketh intercession for the saints according to *the will of* God.
>
> **Revelation 22:12** And, behold, I come quickly; and my reward *is* with me, to give every man according as his work shall be. (Jesus)

Investment Strategy for The Next Life

19 Lay not up for yourselves treasures upon earth, where moth and rust doth corrupt, and where thieves break through and steal:

20 But lay up for yourselves treasures in heaven, where neither moth nor rust doth corrupt, and where thieves do not break through nor steal:

21 For where your treasure is, there will your heart be also.

22 The light of the body is the eye: if therefore thine eye be single, thy whole body shall be full of light.

23 But if thine eye be evil, thy whole body shall be full of darkness. If therefore the light that is in thee be darkness, how great *is* that darkness!

(Continued Next Page)

Spiritual Thoughts

24 No man can serve two masters: for either he will hate the one, and love the other; or else he will hold to the one, and despise the other. Ye cannot serve God and mammon.

Ecclesiastes 5:10 He that loveth silver shall not be satisfied with silver; nor he that loveth abundance with increase: this *is* also vanity.

Proverbs 23:5 Wilt thou set thine eyes upon that which is not? for *riches* certainly make themselves wings; they fly away as an eagle toward heaven.

Revelation 3:18 I counsel thee to buy of me gold tried in the fire, that thou mayest be rich; and white raiment, that thou mayest be clothed, and *that* the shame of thy nakedness do not appear; and anoint thine eyes with eye salve, that thou mayest see.(Jesus)

John 6:27 Labor not for the meat which perisheth, but for that meat which endureth unto everlasting life, which the Son of man shall give unto you: for him hath God the Father sealed. (Jesus)

Proverbs 13:7 There is that maketh himself rich, yet *hath* nothing: *there is* that maketh himself poor, yet *hath* great riches.

1Corinthians 2:14 But the natural man receiveth not the things of the Spirit of God: for they are foolishness unto him: neither can he know *them,* because they are spiritually discerned

Ephesians 4:17 This I say therefore, and testify in the Lord, that ye henceforth walk not as other Gentiles walk, in the vanity of their mind,

having the understanding darkened, being alienated from the life of God through the ignorance that is in them, because of the blindness of their heart:

John 3:19 And this is the condemnation, that light is come into the world, and men loved darkness rather than light, because their deeds were evil.

For every one that doeth evil hateth the light, neither cometh to the light, lest his deeds should be reproved. (Jesus)

James 1:8 A double minded man *is* unstable in all his ways.

Luke 11:23 He that is not with me is against me: and he that gathereth not with me scattereth. (Jesus)

Focus on God's Kingdom, Not This World

25 Therefore I say unto you, Take no thought for your life, what ye shall eat, or what ye shall drink; nor yet for your body, what ye shall put on. Is not the life more than meat, and the body than raiment?

26 Behold the fowls of the air: for they sow not, neither do they reap, nor gather into barns; yet your heavenly Father feedeth them. Are ye not much better than they?

27 Which of you by taking thought can add one cubit unto his stature?

28 And why take ye thought for raiment? Consider the lilies of the field, how they grow; they toil not, neither do they spin:

29 And yet I say unto you, That even Solomon in all his glory was not arrayed like one of these.

Philippians 4:6 Be careful for nothing; but in every thing by prayer and supplication with thanksgiving let your requests be made known unto God.

1Corinthians 9:27 But I keep under my body, and bring *it* into subjection: lest that by any means, when I have preached to others, I myself should be a castaway.

Galatians 5:13 For, brethren, ye have been called unto liberty; only *use* not liberty for an occasion to the flesh, but by love serve one another.

1Peter 3:3-4

3 Whose adorning let it not be that outward *adorning* of plaiting the hair, and of wearing of gold, or of putting on of apparel;

4 But *let it be* the hidden man of the heart, in that which is not corruptible, *even the ornament* of a meek and quiet spirit, which is in the sight of God of great price.

Isaiah 35:1 The wilderness and the solitary place shall be glad for them; and the desert shall rejoice, and blossom as the rose.

Psalms 8:3-6

3 When I consider thy heavens, the work of thy fingers, the moon and the stars, which thou hast ordained;

(Continued Next Page)

Spiritual Thoughts

4 What is man, that thou art mindful of him? and the son of man, that thou visitest him?

5 For thou hast made him a little lower than the angels, and hast crowned him with glory and honor.

6 Thou madest him to have dominion over the works of thy hands; thou hast put all *things* under his feet:

Psalms 139:5-6

5 Thou hast beset me behind and before, and laid thine hand upon me.

6 *Such* knowledge *is* too wonderful for me; it is high, I cannot *attain* unto it.

<u>God Will Provide</u>

30 Wherefore, if God so clothe the grass of the field, which today is, and tomorrow is cast into the oven, *shall he* not much more *clothe* you, O ye of little faith?

31 Therefore take no thought, saying, What shall we eat? or, What shall we drink? or, Wherewithal shall we be clothed?

32 (For after all these things do the Gentiles seek:) for your heavenly Father knoweth that ye have need of all these things.

33 But seek ye first the kingdom of God, and his righteousness; and all these things shall be added unto you.

34 Take therefore no thought for the morrow: for the morrow shall take thought for the things of itself. Sufficient unto the day *is* the evil thereof.

Corinthians 7:31 And they that use this world, as not abusing *it:* for the fashion of this world passeth away.

Matthew 14:20 And they did all eat, and were filled: and they took up of the fragments that remained twelve baskets full.

Colossians 3:2 Set your affection on things above, not on things on the earth.

Deuteronomy 30:9 And the LORD thy God will make thee plenteous in every work of thine hand, in the fruit of thy body, and in the fruit of thy cattle and in the fruit of thy land, for good: for the LORD will again rejoice over thee for good, as he rejoiced over thy fathers:

Luke 12:7 (Jesus) But even the very hairs of your head are all numbered. Fear not therefore: ye are of more value than many sparrows.

Luke 11:10 (Jesus) For every one that asketh receiveth; and he that seeketh findeth; and to him that knocketh it shall be opened.

Luke 12:29 (Jesus) And seek not ye what ye shall eat, or what ye shall drink, neither be ye of doubtful mind.

~~~~~~~~~~~~~~~~~~~~

Matthew 7
Don't Criticize

1 Judge not, that ye be not judged.

2 For with what judgment ye judge, ye shall be judged: and with what measure ye mete, it shall be measured to you again.

3 And why beholdest thou the mote that is in thy brother's eye, but considerest not the beam that *is* in thine own eye?

4 Or how wilt thou say to thy brother, Let me pull out the mote out of thine eye; and, behold, a beam *is* in thine own eye?

5 Thou hypocrite, first cast out the beam out of thine own eye; and then shalt thou see clearly to cast out the mote out of thy brother's eye.

6 Give not that which is holy unto the dogs, neither cast ye your pearls before swine, lest they trample them under their feet, and turn again and rend you.

Romans 2:1 Therefore thou art inexcusable, O man, whosoever thou art that judgest: for wherein thou judgest another, thou condemnest thyself; for thou that judgest doest the same things.

Matthew 25:31-32

31 When the Son of man shall come in his glory, and all the holy angels with him, then shall he sit upon the throne of his glory:

(Continued Next Page)

Spiritual Thoughts

32 And before him shall be gathered all nations: and he shall separate them one from another, as a shepherd divideth *his* sheep from the goats:

Hebrews 2:2 For if the word spoken by angels was steadfast, and every transgression and disobedience received a just recompense of reward;

Hebrews 10:35 Cast not away therefore your confidence, which hath great recompense of reward.

Isaiah 1:16 Wash you, make you clean; put away the evil of your doings from before mine eyes; cease to do evil;

Matthew 13:15 For this people's heart is waxed gross, and *their* ears are dull of hearing, and their eyes they have closed; lest at any time they should see with *their* eyes, and hear with *their* ears, and should understand with *their* heart, and should be converted, and I should heal them.

Directions in Prayer.

7 Ask, and it shall be given you; seek, and ye shall find; knock, and it shall be opened unto you:

8 For every one that asketh receiveth; and he that seeketh findeth; and to him that knocketh it shall be opened.

9 Or what man is there of you, whom if his son ask bread, will he give him a stone?

10 Or if he ask a fish, will he give him a serpent?

11 If ye then, being evil, know how to give good gifts unto your children, how much more shall your Father which is in heaven give good things to them that ask him.

Deuteronomy 4:29 But if from thence thou shalt seek the LORD thy God, thou shalt find *him*, if thou seek him with all thy heart and with all thy soul.

Isaiah 65:24 And it shall come to pass, that before they call, I will answer; and while they are yet speaking, I will hear.

Luke 11:10 For every one that asketh receiveth; and he that seeketh findeth; and to him that knocketh it shall be opened.

Acts 12:5 Peter therefore was kept in prison: but prayer was made without ceasing of the church unto God for him.

Isaiah 64:6 But we are all as an unclean *thing*, and all our righteousnesses *are* as filthy rags; and we all do fade as a leaf; and our iniquities, like the wind, have taken us away.

Isaiah 32:15 Until the spirit be poured upon us from on high, and the wilderness be a fruitful field, and the fruitful field be counted for a forest.

The Golden Principle

12 Therefore all things whatsoever ye would that men should do to you, do ye even so to them: for this is the law and the prophets.

Luke 6:31 (Jesus) And as ye would that men should do to you, do ye also to them likewise.

Deuteronomy 10:12 And now, Israel, what doth the LORD thy God require of thee, but to fear the LORD thy God, to walk in all his ways, and to love him, and to serve the LORD thy God with all thy heart and with all thy soul,

Romans 13:10 Love worketh no ill to his neighbor: therefore love *is* the fulfilling of the law.

John 15:12 (Jesus) This is my commandment, That ye love one another, as I have loved you.

Luke 6:35 (Jesus) But love ye your enemies, and do good, and lend, hoping for nothing again; and your reward shall be great, and ye shall be the children of the Highest: for he is kind unto the unthankful and *to* the evil.

Narrow or Straight?

13 Enter ye in at the strait gate: for wide *is* the gate, and broad *is* the way, that leadeth to destruction, and many there be which go in thereat:

14 Because strait *is* the gate, and narrow *is* the way, which leadeth unto life, and few there be that find it.

15 Beware of false prophets, which come to you in sheep's clothing, but inwardly they are ravening wolves.

(Continued Next Page)

Spiritual Thoughts

16 Ye shall know them by their fruits. Do men gather grapes of thorns, or figs of thistles?

Romans 7:11 For sin, taking occasion by the commandment, deceived me, and by it slew *me*.

Isaiah 28:17 Judgment also will I lay to the line, and righteousness to the plummet: and the hail shall sweep away the refuge of lies, and the waters shall overflow the hiding place.

Philippians 1:27 Only let your conversation be as it becometh the gospel of Christ: that whether I come and see you, or else be absent, I may hear of your affairs, that ye stand fast in one spirit, with one mind striving together for the faith of the gospel;

Proverbs 12:15 The way of a fool *is* right in his own eyes: but he that hearkeneth unto counsel *is* wise.

Luke 18:28-30

28 Then Peter said, Lo, we have left all, and followed thee,

29 And he (Jesus) said unto them, Verily I say unto you, There is no man that hath left house, or parents, or brethren, or wife, or children, for the kingdom of God's sake,

30 Who shall not receive manifold more in this present time, and in the world to come life everlasting.

Revelation 3:4 (Jesus) Thou hast a few names even in Sardis which have not defiled their garments; and they shall walk with me in white: for they are worthy.

Matthew 7:15 (Jesus) Beware of false prophets, which come to you in sheep's clothing, but inwardly they are ravening wolves.

Hebrews 3:12 Take heed, brethren, lest there be in any of you an evil heart of unbelief, in departing from the living God.

James 3:16 For where envying and strife *is*, there *is* confusion and every evil work.

Spiritual Fruit

17 Even so every good tree bringeth forth good fruit; but a corrupt tree bringeth forth evil fruit.

18 A good tree cannot bring forth evil fruit, neither *can* a corrupt tree bring forth good fruit.

19 Every tree that bringeth not forth good fruit is hewn down, and cast into the fire.

20 Wherefore by their fruits ye shall know them.

21 Not every one that saith unto me, Lord, Lord, shall enter into the kingdom of heaven; but he that doeth the will of my Father which is in heaven.

22 Many will say to me in that day, Lord, Lord, have we not prophesied in thy name and in thy name have cast out devils? and in thy name done many wonderful works?

23 And then will I profess unto them, I never knew you: depart from me, ye that work iniquity.

Psalms 92:13 Those that be planted in the house of the LORD shall flourish in the courts of our God.

Matthew 3:10 And now also the axe is laid unto the root of the trees: therefore every tree which bringeth not forth good fruit is hewn down, and cast into the fire.

Revelation 20:12 And I saw the dead, small and great, stand before God; and the books were opened: and another book was opened, which is *the book* of life: and the dead were judged out of those things which were written in the books, according to their works.

2Timothy 3:8-9

8 Now as Jannes and Jambres withstood Moses, so do these also resist the truth: men of corrupt minds, reprobate concerning the faith.

9 But they shall proceed no further: for their folly shall be manifest unto all *men,* as theirs also was.

Psalms 78:35-36

35 And they remembered that God *was* their rock, and the high God their redeemer.

36 Nevertheless they did flatter him with their mouth, and they lied unto him with their tongues.

(Continued Next Page)

Spiritual Thoughts

Luke 8:20-21

20 And it was told him (Jesus) *by certain* which said, Thy mother and thy brethren stand without, desiring to see thee.

21 And he answered and said unto them, My mother and my brethren are these which hear the word of God, and do it.

Galatians 2:16 Knowing that a man is not justified by the works of the law, but by the faith of Jesus Christ, even we have believed in Jesus Christ, that we might be justified by the faith of Christ, and not by the works of the law: for by the works of the law shall no flesh be justified.

Luke 12:9 But he that denies me before men shall be denied before the angels of God.

House Built on the Rock

24 Therefore whosoever heareth these sayings of mine, and doeth them, I will liken him unto a wise man, which built his house upon a rock:

25 And the rain descended, and the floods came, and the winds blew, and beat upon that house; and it fell not; for it was founded upon a rock.

26 And every one that heareth these sayings of mine, and doeth them not, shall be likened unto a foolish man, which built his house upon the sand:

27 And the rain descended, and the floods came, and the winds blew, and beat upon that house; and it fell: and great was the fall of it.

1Corinthians 3:11 For other foundation can no man lay than that is laid, which is Jesus Christ.

Romans 5:3-5

3 And not only *so,* but we glory in tribulations also: knowing that tribulation worketh patience;

4 And patience, experience; and experience, hope:

5 And hope maketh not ashamed; because the love of God is shed abroad in our hearts by the Holy Ghost which is given unto us.

Psalms 91:5 Thou shalt not be afraid for the terror by night; *nor* for the arrow *that* flieth by day;

Hebrews 2:2 For if the word spoken by angels was steadfast, and every transgression and disobedience received a just recompense of reward;

James 2:14 What *doth it* profit, my brethren, though a man say he hath faith, and have not works? can faith save him?

James 4:17 Therefore to him that knoweth to do good, and doeth *it* not, to him it is sin.

Amos 8:14 They that swear by the sin of Samaria, and say, Thy god O Dan, liveth; and, The manner of Beer-sheba liveth; even they shall fall, and never rise up again.

www.ingramcontent.com/pod-product-compliance
Lightning Source LLC
Chambersburg PA
CBHW022357040426
42450CB00005B/229